GW01086504

London's
Mounted Police
1960 to 2000

Cover Picture: The Author riding 'point' on the Mounted Branch Grey Escort on police horse 'Kathleen' on the occasion of the state visit of the President of Turkey, 1989

Back cover picture: Police horse 'Casa Mayor'. Picture courtesy of Mike Pattison Photography, Hainault.

London's
Mounted Police
1960 to 2000

A mounted policeman's memories

Andy Petter

Published by www.lulu.com

© Copyright Andrew Petter 2017
Cartoons by Richard Duszac of Cartoon Studios Ltd. are the
exclusive copyright of Andy Petter

LONDON'S
MOUNTED POLICE
1960 TO 2000

All rights reserved.

The right of Andrew Petter to be identified as the author of this
work has been asserted in accordance with the Copyright, Designs
and Patents Act 1988.

No part of this publication may be reproduced, stored in a retrieval
system, or transmitted, in any form or by any means, electronic,
mechanical, photocopying, recording or otherwise, nor translated
into a machine language, without the written permission of the
publisher.

Condition of sale

This book is sold subject to the condition that it shall not, by way
of trade or otherwise, be lent, re-sold, hired out or otherwise
circulated in any form of binding or cover other than that in which
it is published and without a similar condition including this
condition being imposed on the subsequent purchaser.

ISBN 978-1-326-99053-4

Book formatted by www.bookformatting.co.uk.

Contents

Comment

This memoir is unique in that it's the first time that a long serving Mounted Police officer has laid down his thoughts and perspective of events during an exceptional busy and challenging time for the Metropolitan Police.

London's Mounted Branch was made up of a strength of over 200 horses, nearly double the strength of today's force. This account details the author's early life in the tranquil valleys of the South Downs through a hilarious account of his National Service with the King's Troop Royal Horse Artillery at St John's Wood during the late 50's and his early, almost Dickensian years on the beat in East London where the notorious gangs of the Krays and The Richardsons were making life very interesting for the beat bobby.

Andy Petter was a raw recruit when first posted to Stoke Newington at a time where personal radios and mobile phones were non existent. There were no traffic wardens and the Met's total strength was less than 15000 with very little civilian support.

His early account of life on the beat together with his anecdotal exchanges with the public make for amusing and revealing information of just, 'getting by' with the minimum of technological support. The great support he got from both his colleagues, senior officers and the general public more than replaced any shortfall of equipment, though looking back it seems impossible that they had so little.

His later account of progress through the Mounted Branch at virtually every area in London details a remarkable career where political upheaval and terrorism brought him into contact with tragedy and chaos.

For the equestrian there are hilarious accounts of cussed horses with mean streaks that should never have been on the streets to gentle solid and lovable characters that gave lifelong service to a force that sometimes forgot their loyalty.

Sit back then and enjoy this account of a different world to every day life and witness the contribution made to London life by the Police Horse.

Foreword

Many thoughts crossed my mind before I embarked upon writing this account of my life in 'London's Mounted Branch and before'. It always seemed to me that there was a certain vanity in laying down the events in one's life to paper, after all the world is full of interesting people all of whom have an interesting tale to tell and the world would soon fill up with the paper of unread life histories if every one took up the pen.

My life was no different to many others, yet upon reflection I so wish my Father had kept a diary or written an article about his experiences through two world wars when he served as a Royal Marine. He spoke very little of his time in uniform and I never took the trouble to closely quiz him while he was alive.

Looking back I wished I had teased the account from him regarding his feelings as a young Nineteen year old Gunner in the Marine Artillery when he sailed on the 'Revenge' in 1916 to take on the German Fleet at 'The Battle of Jutland'. What thoughts were going through his young head as their massive guns blazed away at the enemy or more to the point what were his thoughts as they blazed away at the British Fleet? Or when, as a 43 year old Father of five children being recalled for a second world war and his thoughts when being bombarded in Bari Docks in Italy in December 1943.

How interesting it would be if families had a written account of their ancestor's experiences through their lives. In today's modern age of computerized technology every one is using the genealogy sites in the hope of picking up some unusual item but we are lucky if we can find out much more than where they lived, their occupation and cause of death. How much more interesting it would be for our descendents if their forefathers had been given the opportunity to pass on a record of their lives!

Of course a diary is one way of keeping such a record but would scarcely survive a Generation or two, but I suggest a book would be far more durable, particularly if it covers a particularly interesting or exciting period. A book would also serve as a record of events as seen by the author whose experiences may be very different from the Media's account.

In my own career of 35 years of service with the Metropolitan Police of which over thirty were served at all ranks within the Mounted Branch I can think of many incidents that would give a valuable insight into the work and changing nature of policing on horseback during a very volatile period.

I was fortunate enough to be serving at a time when The Metropolitan Police had over 200 horses. They were readily deployed to control large crowds and maintain order in volatile situations. My period of service covered events from as early as Sir Winston Churchill's Funeral in 1965, through riots at Grosvenor Square, Red Lion Square, Greenham Common, Wapping and many more up to my retirement in 1994.

It was quite common to turn out 120 Horses or more throughout London on a Saturday or Sunday on football matches and various public order events. Most of the time such policing was performed with the full support of the public, with whom for the most part we enjoyed a happy relationship. The average Mounted Police Officer after 2 or 3 years was selected as a specialist and expected to serve a lifetime within the Branch. Consequently a great spirit of comrade-ship and professionalism developed. There was much good work performed and although there were difficult times particularly with riots and terrorism, a unique sense of humour was always present.

It's these events and anecdotes that I put to paper in the hope that they can be found interesting and enjoyable not only by my immediate family but also as an individual account of life for London's Mounted Policemen and Women through a most challenging period.

To my lifelong love and wife Christine
and my two lovely children, Yvonne and Richard
who have added so much support and joy to my life.

To Gerry Hanson and Helen Cope for their support and
encouragement.

Chapter One

Fortress Wapping

The line of Police Horses were mainly well behaved as they stood about 20 yards behind the Shield Serials, some moved restlessly as the debris of rocks, tiles and house bricks found their way through or past the perspex shields and shattered round their feet. The noise was deafening as gangs of hooded rioters wearing balaclavas hurled abuse and rocks at the police lines.

It was Saturday 24th January 1987. The location was Wapping Highway and tonight was to be the last desperate attempt by Rupert Murdoch's print workers to wreck his new print operation in Wapping.

Most of the horses were solid police horses, experienced in public order and had been attending the Wapping dispute for nearly a year. I was fortunate to be riding an outstanding police horse who was completely relaxed in spite of the furore. I knew he would be completely fearless once we commenced the crowd dispersal. A former Grand National and Cheltenham Gold Cup' runner, 'Casa Mayor' would take this event in his stride.

Above all the noise and activity I was aware of the Ground Commander grabbing my riding boot to get my attention. 'We're going to have to hang on until the DAC gets here to take a look, maybe another 20 minutes.' he shouted in my ear as I leant forward in the saddle. 'He'll need to be quick; these guys can't take much more.' I shouted back, 'if they break through the cordon we'll have to get stuck in.'

The previous two hours has seen enormous police activity with the foot duty making snatch arrests and holding back violent charges by the mob. Near exhaustion and needing some relief it was obvious that Mounted Branch would soon be deployed if we were to regain the initiative.

I had already completed my briefing so that every mounted officer knew we were about to disperse the mob. Warnings had been broadcast to the crowd, the Shield Serial Chief Inspector had prepared his officers that we were about to come between them, With 23 Horses at our disposal it was just a case of waiting for deployment.

I looked round at the four rows of horses and noticed how all the officers had removed their high visibility jackets. My Sergeant, on his bright chestnut, was immediately to my left as we stood in the front line. 'Not a job for long sticks Sarge' I said, referring to the long batons we carried. 'No, I'll be happier with both hands on the reins for this one Sir' he replied with commendable determination.

The street wasn't wide enough to take more than about eight horses in line and I could see my Inspector some two rows back in command of the rear lines.

I saw the district assistant commissioner talking with the Ground Commander as they surveyed the scene and then he turned to me and gave the signal I had been waiting for. I nodded to the Shield Serial Chief Inspector and he instantly gave the command for his men to split as we moved between their lines and into the mob.

Chapter Two
Early Years

If I had been told as a young boy reared in the tranquil valley of Milland in West Sussex, that one day I would be riding in tight formation with a group of Mounted Police Officers clad in body armour upon steeds wearing protective visors and leg guards into a mob of missile throwing rioters bent on arson and violence, I doubt that I would ever have left home.

As it was, my career and events had determined that such was to be the case and looking back now I am grateful for the opportunity to be involved in such challenging and interesting times.

My early schooldays at Wardly Primary School and later at Midhurst Grammar School were mainly with children from an agricultural background, although my Father had served as a regular Royal Marine during two world wars, we were very much a family living within a farming community.

Born in January 1940, I was the youngest of five children and to my parents astonishment arrived some seven months after the loss of my twin sibling complete with a Caul or Cowl which the Mid Wife assured my distraught Mother was a sign of luck and nothing to worry about.

I think I must have had a guilt complex regarding my survival as for several of my early years I had occasional macabre nightmares where I felt responsible for my twins loss. I think the idea might have been implanted in my brain by my nine year old brother peeking over the cot and whispering 'Murderer' when no else was about.

Being so young I remember very little of the war years, though I can remember soldiers living under the hedges around Milland as they prepared for 'D day landings'. We sometimes encountered long columns of military vehicles along the leafy roads to Petersfield as we caught the twice-daily bus service that ran between Petersfield and Midhurst. I can distinctly remember being woken in the middle of the night by the droning of hundreds of aircraft as they flew over Milland to the south coast on their bombing raids to Germany. Later that night or probably the following morning I would again wake to hear the sound of the survivors returning.

But looking back apart from the foregoing I realize that my childhood was idyllic. My earliest recollection of horses was to stand with my two sisters at the barn door while we watched the farrier shoe Mr. Clue's Shire horse, though I cannot remember if I ever saw it in harness.

I would have been about three or four years of age and remember being pulled back by my sisters when I innocently responded to the Farriers' laughing request for one of us to hold the animal's hind foot while he nailed the shoe on. At the time the horse's hoof was bigger than my head.

I'm not suggesting that the farming community relied on shire horses to plough their fields and gather the crops, far from it, the Fordson tractor was the carthorse of the day and later the farmers favoured the Ferguson, working horses were not the norm in 1944.

We never kept horses but one of my school friends owned a horse. We would have been about twelve when I used to accompany him for miles on foot while he rode round Redford Common just for the chance of a few minutes in the saddle. He was a lively New Forest pony and I remember the exhilaration of my first rising trot and canter around the village green.

Life was pretty idyllic with what seemed like endless games of softball Cricket and Football. Dad was home from the war and working for the local council. We had little money but sufficient to feed and clothe five children and pay the rent of 10 shillings (50p) a week for a semi detached three bedroomed cottage, with a large

4

garden full of vegetables. We kept hens and rabbits to supplement Dad's small income and although we kept pets we could never afford a pony or horse. My Mother was a wonderful and resourceful cook and top rate seamstress. She was able to unpick used shirts, reverse cuffs and adapt hand me downs so that you would think the clothes were new.

I managed to scrape a place at Midhurst Grammar School when I passed the eleven plus. We went to Sunday School in Milland and our Mum would take us to our local Church at Iping Marsh where I did my best to sing in the choir.

I would have been about ten or eleven when I first encountered a police officer. Every night I would walk the family Cocker Spaniel past the Rising Sun public house to the fields beyond and often as I passed the only phone box for miles, a solitary Constable would be waiting alongside his Velocette motorbike. Looking back he was probably waiting to ring his base or for them to ring him for of course there were no personal radios or mobile phones in the 1950's.

To me he seemed to be an authoritive figure with a public duty to perform whilst at the same time reasonably approachable. Sometimes we would exchange a word or two if I could summon up the courage to say hello. I think it was as early as this that I decided to join the Force. I was extremely proud of my father's long service with the Royal Marines through two world wars and both of my older brothers had also joined. But such is the nature of things where children often break with family tradition and encouraged by my Mother; I resolved to join the Metropolitan Police.

Chapter Three

A Case To Answer

'Hello Andrew, it's Margaret, how are the ribs?'

'Hi Margaret, OK, they must be getting better, but if I move at night it wakes me up.'

It was my Sister and just one week after the barrage at Wapping. We had 23 horses and 22 officers injured that night and I had caught a full house brick under my right arm and collected two broken ribs in the process.

'Well I've been reading that there's to be a full enquiry and that a lot of you are likely to be charged with criminal offences.'

'Well that's right about the enquiry and many of us have been served formal notices of complaints against us.'

'Well where does that leave you, will you be charged?' Margaret was my older sister by three years and had always taken it upon herself to look after me ever since I could remember.

'Don't worry; we always get a big enquiry after Mounted Branch are deployed in a riot. It was the same at Red Lion Square and at Southall where Blair Peach was killed. It's just another follow up to a big event where there's been a lot of injuries.'

'Well it looks a bit more than that according to the press, are you in the clear?'

'Well, I've received notice that I've got several complaints against me personally which is a bit unusual but I know we did a good job and acted correctly. I'm being interviewed by the investigating team next week; I'll let you know how it goes.'

She's right I thought as I put the phone down. This enquiry is a bit more than the usual investigation that follows a deployment of Mounted Police.

Many, if not all of the Mounted Officers on duty that night had been formally served with forms 163, something that didn't happen very often within the Mounted Branch. One of the purposes of the form was to ensure that the officers were fully aware of the complaints made against them. I had received no less than five complaints following our deployment at Wapping. As the Senior Mounted Officer in charge I had naturally received the bulk of the complaints. Nevertheless the rest of the Mounted Personnel had received at least one complaint ranging from 'Excessive force in using Mounted Issue long truncheons' to 'Riding to the danger of the public.'

I had received the following complaint filed by Chief Superintendent Wyrko of the Northampton Police Investigation team.

In September 1987 The Haldane Society of Socialist Lawyers published their report on the policing of the news International demonstration at Wapping on Saturday 24th January, 1987 called, A Case to Answer? In that report allegations are made concerning the manner of deployment of the police horses in that the horses galloped through the people assembled in Wellclose Street without stopping until they reached the Union Bus (A reference to a stationary vehicle used by union members for comfort Etc.) It is alleged that this is in breach of ACPO guidelines.

From enquiries conducted into these complaints and allegations it would appear that officers under your command were in possession of equipment (namely riding whips) not issued officially to operational officers and were allowed to use this equipment during the course of the mounted deployments.'

The complaint then listed complaints from seven different sources raging from;

Charging at the crowd at a gallop.

Indiscriminate manner in which the horses charged into the crowd.

Unnecessary Deployment of Police Horses.

To:-

Discreditable conduct, neglect of duty and abuse of authority.

I was absolutely certain that our action was correct and that we had nothing to fear from any inquiry. On the night in question foot duty serials had taken an unbearable amount of hostility and physical injury for a period of over two hours. The print works that we were protecting were in danger of being overrun with great risks to staff and property. The demonstrators had taken their action far beyond reasonable picketing and by their actions shown that they were bent on violence and disorder.

We had taken great care to act within ACPO guidelines in use of horses for crowd dispersal, namely that we had broadcast by loud hailer that the crowd must disperse or we would have to deploy horses and that when we advanced upon the crowd we did so in a manner that met with the approval of the Association of Chief Police Officers and the Home Office.

The Police Federation had been very supportive and took very little time to arrange for legal representation. Lawyers agreed we had nothing to fear from any inquiry and that our action was correct and commendable whilst preventing further injury and damage.

Nevertheless they felt it would be wise to refrain from making any statement and wait to see the nature of any possible action that might be brought against us. Unfortunately this was later to be regarded by the media as though we had something to hide. Indeed the opposite was the case and the Mounted Branch to a man was proud of their action that night, many were bemused by the fact that they had not received recognition for doing such a good job.

Being of Chief Inspector rank, my representation was dealt with by a different member of the Police Federation. I had already put my thoughts to paper during the week's sickness following the event and had a fully prepared statement ready for any interview with the inquiry team from Northamptonshire. I was so glad that I did for I was later to discover from Assistant Commissioner Geofrey McClean at Scotland Yard that my statement was very helpful to the Met in countering the assertions from the press that we were involved in a cover up.

That night on the 24th January 1987 was the last night of the Printers Dispute following a year of picketing, violence and hostility between pickets and workers. The Metropolitan Police had been the buffer in the middle and as such ensured that proper order prevailed.

In the weeks and months that were to follow I never once worried that our action was anything other than fully justified under the circumstances. My sister Margaret, bless her, would continue to worry on my behalf until the report was published but the work of the Mounted Branch would carry on regardless of the events at Wapping.

Chapter Four
Police Cadets, Hendon & First Posting

My first introduction to London's Mounted Branch was most unusual. I had arrived in the big city from the pastures and woodlands of West Sussex as a sixteen year old during the month of August 1956 for my interview for the Police Cadets. The interview required the candidates to report to the Metropolitan Police recruiting centre at Beak Street in Soho. The furthest I had ever travelled from my sleepy village of Milland was to visit my aunt on the Isle of Wight, now here I was accommodated for the night in the heart of the capital while awaiting interview and medical the following day.

Three or four of us hopeful candidates decided to make the most of our first time in London by taking a walk round the sights and not waste any time by sitting around in the Police Section House. It was late evening and dark when we eventually found ourselves in Parliament Square. We decided to walk down Whitehall to Trafalgar Square. As we approached Downing Street we found our way blocked by a large crowd of excitable people chanting anti government slogans regarding the Suez crisis and giving the Police cordons a hard time. We were advised by a friendly Police Constable who quickly saw that we were not your average tourist or protester, 'If you want to make your interview tomorrow lads you'd best make yourselves scarce' and promptly sent us off in the direction of the embankment to avoid the demonstration.

We cheerfully diverted our route and were further astonished to see a long column of Mounted Police trotting (some cantering) along the embankment in the direction we had just left. It was my first sight of London's Mounted Branch in action. At the time we thought this was an every day occurrence, it was the following day that we learnt that the crowd we had seen earlier had overrun the Police cordons in Downing Street and were threatening the doors of the Prime Minister. In those days there were no high metal railings for protection and anyone could stand outside Number 10 and take a picture of the sole Constable on duty outside the famous black door.

In the coming months and years I was to speak with many of the officers who had been on duty that night. It transpired that once the foot duty had lost control of the situation a detachment of Mounted Officers who had been on standby at Great Scotland Yard had been called into action to break up the crowd and move them away from Downing Street. In the melee one of the Mounted Officers had become dismounted and injured. Most unusually his place was promptly taken by a foot duty Constable, PC Maurice Dent, who having earlier riding experience sprang into the saddle and worked with the other Mounted Officers in crowd clearance.

Needless to say, Maurice soon found himself a successful applicant for the Branch and on the Six Month Mounted Training course at Imber Court, a good talking point for the selection panel but a most unusual way of bringing himself to notice. Maurice was a popular Officer and served for several years before leaving to run a successful garage business in Esher.

My interview for the cadets was successful and on the 16th August 1956, I reported to Hendon Training School for one month's training before being transferred to the Mounted Branch Administration offices in the old bungalow building at New Scotland Yard known by its departmental code as A5. I was little more than an office boy in uniform for the next seven months though we did see a change of scenery, when the whole office transferred to new quarters above the stables at Great Scotland Yard.

All of the buildings around Whitehall have a history and Great Scotland Yard was no exception. It was unique in that it had been custom built for the Right Honorable Cecil Lowther, Earl of

Lonsdale in 1911/12. Its main feature was that the horses were housed on the first floor whilst the ground floor was for carriages. The two upper floors were for Grooms accommodation but had since been converted into offices.

To get to the first floor the horses used an inclined ramp, which was carpeted with coconut matting to prevent slipping. Once on the first floor the stables were split into two, with the front section overlooking the street and accommodated about ten loose boxes. The rear stable was without exterior windows and had stalls for a further ten horses. The whole complex would have been very gloomy if it hadn't been for a huge suspended glass roof which allowed light into the interior.

Our new offices were two further floors above the stable, right at the very top of the building. This small office complex was composed of an office for the head of the Mounted Branch, Chief Superintendent Dai Bowen, Station Police Sergeant (SPS) Gordon Hicks one Police Constable Dennis Maxwell and one other Police Cadet Derek Bryson.

My duties were fairly comfortable although for two months before Christmas 1956 we were lumbered with counting and dispatching the force Christmas cards and envelopes for the whole of the Metropolitan police, probably about 100,000 cards. Other duties included typing, using the old Roneo or Gestetner copying machines, keeping the coal burning fires going, answering the telephone and making the tea.

Having just arrived from the wilds of West Sussex, any spare moment was spent down stairs in the stables where I was quickly coerced into cleaning tack, swinging chains and grooming the odd horse. It was like home from home for me, the horses always seemed to be immaculate and I found it rewarding to work around them.

In 1956 National Service was still a requirement for all fit young men, (Not Women, would you believe.) However, after about 1954 certain occupations including the Police Service were exempt. It was while I was serving at A5 that I first heard of how previous Police Cadets had been able to join The King's Troop Royal Horse

Artillery at St John's Wood for their National Service. This stood them in good stead for joining the Mounted Branch at a later date. Although I was in an exempt category as a Police Cadet, I discovered that if I wanted, I could still volunteer for National Service. This meant that a recruit would only serve for two years rather than the regular army recruit who had to sign on for a minimum 3 years. For someone who was bored with office life and looking at another 18 months of the same, the chance of joining a horsed unit and gaining a top quality riding ability was very attractive. It would mean working for a quarter of the wages but my food and accommodation would be included. Looking back on the situation 50 years later I am convinced that I must have been brain washed by the Mounted Officers at Great Scotland Yard to take such a step.

Consequently my Chief Superintendent, Dai Bowen, arranged for me to attend an interview with the Adjutant of The King's Troop RHA at St. John's Wood. This impressive Captain tried to persuade me to sign up for the Military Police or failing that perhaps a post as a regimental police officer. But I was having none of it, I left him in no doubt that I would only join as a jockey or I would stay a police cadet until being made a constable in eighteen Months or so, I was only joining for the experience with horses.

I left the Barracks that evening with a letter of introduction to present to the recruiting officer when I went for my medical at Wanstead. Apparently it wasn't that easy to get into the King's Troop without previous riding experience unless one signed on for at least a three-year term. The selection Officer at Wanstead again tried to convince me that the Military Police should be my route but once he saw my letter of introduction agreed to my transfer to The King's Troop Royal Horse Artillery once I had completed my initial training.

Chapter Five

National Service

So at the tender age of 17years and 8 Months and after only 9 Months service as a Police Cadet I found myself, the only person born in 1940 to perform National Service, on a northbound train to the Royal Artillery training camp at Oswestry in Shropshire. We were met at the station by various service personal before being loaded onto an ageing double decker bus to convey us to the barracks. We were then kitted out with uniform and given a meal before being instructed to write home (by order) to let our parents know we had arrived safe and sound.

The next two weeks didn't seem very safe and sound at all. We were marched from pillar to post, given basic training in use of the old Lee Enfield 303 rifle and physical training with super fit amazons who took perverse pleasure in chasing us across logs, rivers, climbing ropes and crawling under tarpaulins. I must admit that in those first two weeks I thought I had made a big mistake; surely I had joined to perform most of these acts on horseback. But we ate and slept very well and after two weeks we were on our way to our respective Units.

I was somewhat alarmed to find my rail ticket was booked to Okehampton in Devon. Looking back, I cannot remember what I expected other than returning to St John's Wood in a fashionable part of London. Instead there was I complete with full kitbag and standard issue army rations with two other confused Squaddys heading for the wilds of Dartmoor. Over the next few hours we were to learn much about each other's former lives. Both of my travelling companions had previous experience with horses in one form or another. One was an apprentice harness and saddle maker while the other was an apprentice jockey. The latter had already ridden in 5 races, all of which, he ruefully informed us he had finished last though he claimed to be 'Only riding to Orders.'

But where we were going was a mystery, we all thought we should be heading for London but resigned ourselves to accepting the Army's 'need to know' philosophy, clearly they thought that we didn't.

Eventually we arrived at the sleepy village of Oakhampton in Devon where a friendly ticket collector seemed to know what we were there for and what to do. He instructed us to wait outside the station and wait for Army transport. It was a hot sunny August afternoon. After two weeks of being chased from dawn to dusk at Oswestry, we suddenly felt Army life was pretty good after all. Our contentment was soon shattered by the arrival of an Army Bedford truck which was to take us on the final leg of our journey.

All three of us weighed little more than 9 stone each and the friendly driver was quite happy for us all to cram into the front cab with him. Throwing our kit bags into the back of the truck he set off for the moors of Devon. The scenery was beautiful as we drove across the moors under Yes Tor. The driver explained that 'Yes' we had come to join The King's Troop Royal Horse Artillery and agreed that 'No' this wasn't St John's Wood London NW8 but the Army's Southern Command Battle ground and the King's Troop were at Summer Camp or 'Schemes' on the Moors for three weeks.

After driving along moorland paths and across many cattle grids we finally emerged onto an open area, which was obviously a Field Army Camp. We were left outside a tent in which there were four bunk beds, this was to be our home for the remaining two weeks of camp. The place was deserted apart from one cook, a blacksmith and a couple of horses. It transpired that the rest of the Troop had split up into three groups and all disappeared out onto the Moors for three days on what was referred to as 'Schemes'. I was later to learn that 'Schemes' was a reference to living rough on the moors with your horses, making do with what ever shelter you could find.

The whole camp couldn't have numbered more than ten people and after being given a meal we were left to settle in and prepare for the return of the Troop the following day.

'Preparing for the Troop the following day' transpired to be cookhouse fatigues where we had to peel a mountain of spuds for chips for 100 inbound hungry Soldiers who had just ridden off the moors.

As they came back in small groups I was struck by how small the horses were compared to the Police Horses I had left in London. The King's Troop horses existed for the sole purpose of pulling a gun and limber weighing well over a ton at speed. Consequently they were only about 15 hands, short powerful and very fit. The riders were all dressed in khaki Army service uniform with breeches and puttees. No riding boots for the squaddy just rolled khaki bandages around the lower leg. There were a few immaculate riding boots to be seen however. These belonged to the Commissioned Officers, more elegantly dressed than the squaddys. Their bearing was one of supervisor as the soldiers went about securing their horses. By the end of the afternoon about a hundred horses had returned to camp and were happily munching their oats while we all found ourselves eating a few of the potatoes we had been preparing all morning.

After a day or two we made our way back to Okehampton Train Station where at a railway siding we helped load all the horses onto cattle carriages to stand side by side across the vehicle. Their heads faced wooden slats with small gaps on one side, with their tails against the other. Any stroppy horses, 'biters or kickers', of which there were surprisingly few, were accommodated in plush padded individual compartments that were also designated for Officers Chargers. (It seemed to me that the Officer status also extended to their horses.) There were eight horses to each carriage and they all had a hay net each, They all seemed content as the train moved off but there was much amusement after about half an hour on our way to London when we looked out of the carriage window to see about 100 tails happily flying in a 60 mile an hour breeze.

Some few hours later we pulled into Olympia railway sidings. This was to be the first time of many when I saw these wonderful little gun horses happily standing in batches of three with just one rider on the centre horse leading the two outside horses. The riders were dressed in breeches and puttees and with a minimum of fuss set off for their permanent barracks in St John's Wood North London some four miles away.

I quickly learnt that the practice of riding one horse and leading two was commonly known as 'Rough Exercise', something that I was to become very familiar with over the next two years and something which gave the horseman a very safe and balanced seat under the most demanding of riding conditions. With only an army blanket for a saddle held in place with a single strap and the lightest of snaffles for control one quickly learnt the art of balance and control through London's busy streets, something that stood me in such good stead for my forthcoming years working in London's Mounted Police. The secret of a comfortable ride was to make sure you rode the most rounded horse of your three, a narrow backed horse would cut you in two.

The everyday routine at St John's Wood varied throughout the year depending on State Ceremonial events or preparing for, or taking part in their famous musical drive at The Royal Tournament and various show grounds around the country. The Troop had about 100 horses, which before arriving at St John's Wood, were partly 'broken in' at the Remount Training Depot in Melton Mowbray.

We were assigned to one of the six subsections made up of 16 men to each Sub. I was posted to 'C' Sub. I quickly learnt that without exception all of my buddies had extensive previous experience with horses. Some were apprentice jockeys; others had been working in Hunt Stables or Riding Schools.

In 1957 The King's Troop riding school was only half the size it is today,[1] the original school had been magnificent but converted so that half of the building was used to accommodate an admin block and harness rooms. The only other riding area was a small outdoor ménage and an exercise track round the parade square. This limited riding area meant that a lot of the exercise was performed on the streets. Reveille was 6am followed by frantic cleaning out of the stables before going on parade at 6.30 with about 70 horses in rough exercise order, viz. one rider to three horses equipped only with snaffle and saddle blanket. Once formed up and ready to leave an officer, normally a junior Lieutenant would emerge from the officer's mess and mount his waiting horse before leading a three hundred foot long column out onto the streets of North West London.

The rough exercise always took a varied route, one day we would be clattering up the Finchley Road whilst on another we could be in Bayswater. Hampstead Heath was another route but wherever we went it wasn't long before the horses were steaming with exertion. Most of the horses were seasoned, obedient and happy to go with the flow. There would always be one or two who

---

[1] Authors note. At the time of writing the King's Troop were still stationed at St John's Wood, The Troop has since been moved to new barracks at Woolwich.

would like to show off, either through inexperience or sheer enthusiasm they would throw a display of bucking and kicking that would impress a Spanish Riding School instructor, especially if any passing vehicles got too close.

The secret of a comfortable ride was to select the most rounded horse and keep going forward no matter what. The long trail of horses was not to be split. For example at traffic lights, once the officer committed us to crossing we never stopped, Further down the line the lights would change to red but we never stopped. To do so was to invite chaos, the delayed horses would have none of it and to try and restrain them keeping up with their mates would see them perform all kinds of gymnastics.

We always made a point of keeping together though God help us if we allowed our horses to get so close to the three in front that we trod on their heels. Apart from the following dressing down from the NCO on return to barracks, a tread would normally lead to the injured horses booting out at the culprit.

Occasionally such disruption caused chaos and the odd loose horse was not unknown, on one occasion about eight horses escaped and were seen happily cantering along Oxford Street pursued by Army personnel, cab drivers and police alike. Some we managed to catch, but at least two had to be collected from the police station yard at West End Central.

Later I overheard a rueful Bombardier who had been sent to retrieve them, complaining that he had to sign for them before the Met. Police would release them.

Although this was a time when Britain was approaching the end of National Service, there were still many young men born before 1940 caught in that catchment period which meant they had to leave their homes and budding careers to do their bit for 'King and Country' by serving for two years. Indeed, many National Service Men had seen action in Korea, Kenya, Suez and many other theatres of war. Consequently all service units saw a high turnover of staff. The riding school was testament to that. Class after class would be brought up to a good standard before going on to ride in the gun teams or detachment and then de-mobbed after two years.

We were very fortunate to have two excellent riding instructors in Sergeant Ben Jones, who later went on to win an Olympic Gold Medal in the Three Day Event in Mexico and Bombardier Eric Witts. Both men had vast experience with horses before joining the Troop but were also excellent instructors. Not that we had an easy time in riding school, just the opposite, but after four weeks we went from novice to a competency which allowed us to ride rough exercise around the streets with some degree of safety.

Barrack room life and Army discipline soon saw a comradeship develop. The Army in 1956 was an all male environment, the only females at that time were in the women's only regiments such as the Woman's Royal Army Corps and we never came into contact with any other regiments apart from the time the Para's raided our lines whilst on schemes in Yorkshire. They set our horses free in the middle of the night and made off with half our harness. The following day saw much negotiation between our officers and theirs before the harness was returned. Of course a raid on their camp three nights later saw us making off with their cookhouse equipment.

The days seemed long and in addition we were required to work additional shifts through the night on guard duty. The barracks had at all times to be kept immaculate. With straw blowing in all directions and regular horse droppings on the parade ground our lives spent a lot of time behind the broom. One day together with another gunner from my sub-section we found ourselves sweeping the paths adjoining the Officer Mess. Gunner Glasby with dour Yorkshire wit managed to sweep his way up to the window of the splendid lounge with a view to gaze at the crystal chandeliers and mess silver on the mahogany tables. Batmen were laying out the dining room with pristine linen napkins and fine china. Sweeping his way back to me I had to laugh at his broad Yorkshire comment. 'My God. They live like fooking Lords, don't they!' There certainly was a big contrast between the various messes for different ranks.

Nevertheless we were all in our late teens or early twenty's with high spirits and I was soon to learn about the initiation for all new recruits when one December evening another new recruit and I was informed that we better get some Denims on as we were about to be "Troughed".

Chapter Six
King's Troop Initiation

Now "Troughing" as the word implies had something to do with the deep watering troughs provided for 'Watering Order' or the watering of ten horses at a time, three times a day. At set times; horses which normally stood tethered to the wall on either side of an aisle were untied and turned inwards to face each other. We would stand with two horses each waiting to lead out to the yard and stand in line before the trough waiting for the Bombardier to give the order to 'lead on' at the sounding of a trumpet. Even the horses got used to Army discipline and knew they couldn't charge onto the trough without the order.

However these troughs were also used for another function in that they were used for an initiation ceremony into the troop. It was a well-known fact that no one could claim to be a Soldier in the King's Troop without being dunked in these deep troughs. However one was expected to fight and not submit although the outcome was inevitable. I resolved that when my turn came I would take a few with me.

The Barracks stood on about 4 Acres of land surrounded by a high brick wall dating back to the Victorian period. It housed not only accommodation for 120 gunners and 90 horses but also a riding school, gun park, parade ground and all the other ancillary support buildings compatible with an Army Troop. We were confined to Barracks unless issued with a pass and all gates were guarded by our own soldiers. This meant that the area of chase was limited.

Warning for the initiation was always given with the words 'get your denims (Work Fatigues) on, we'll give you ten minutes.' On the evening my turn came around I was warned with another friend who had joined the Troop a couple of weeks before me Dennis (Brandy) Bridges.

We both shot off to get changed and then with no idea where to hide, headed off across the parade ground towards the horse lines. Dennis made for the old clock tower above the riding school while I was delighted to see a fire hose rapidly filling one of the troughs. Wishing to spoil my pursuer's fun as much as I could I dived into the trough and grabbed the hose. Now I had some artillery and as the mob rounded the corner let them have full pressure as they closed in.

Needless to say I emerged ten minutes later half drowned but triumphant that I had got the lot of them. Meanwhile Brandy was keeping them at bay from his refuge high up in the tower by hurling old boxes, sacks, horse shoes and anything else that came to hand before he ran out of missiles and was captured and similarly half drowned.

This initiation was completely classless and extended to NCOs Warrant Officers and Commissioned Officers alike.[2]

---

[2] (Authors note. I recently returned to the barracks after a 50-year absence and found that the troughs have been removed and horses now have individual automatic watering mangers. I was reliably informed that the ancient initiation ceremony of 'Troughing' has been vanquished to history and that new intakes are now simply thrown into the dung heap.)

Chapter Seven
Royal Salutes And Gun Teams

Over the next two years as our standard of riding improved I graduated from a complete riding novice to an accomplished horseman. The main purpose of the troop as a ceremonial unit was to fire Royal Salutes on State Occasions. The King's Troop was a half battery and a ceremonial salute involved riding from St John's Wood to Hyde Park with six 13 pounder guns and limbers pulled by teams of 6 horses, each team was followed by a detachment of 3 horses and riders whose purpose was to dismount at the scene of the royal salute and unhook and fire the guns.

The gun salutes were a terrific spectacle and would draw large crowds of spectators. The salute took the form of forming up six teams abreast, galloping North to South on a parallel course with Park Lane for about two furlongs of Hyde Park before unhooking the guns ready for firing while the horses and limbers retreated to a safe distance.

Now many of the horses had characters of their own and one such horse in our sub-section was number 26 'Peter' He was a lovely horse to ride with great enthusiasm and prepared to tackle anything. Apart from being one of the miscreants who escaped in Oxford Street, he also managed to escape in Hyde Park during a royal salute. Having escaped from the detachment Peter felt his place was back with the unhooked guns which were in place and ready to fire. Although we only fired blank shells, they nevertheless packed quite a charge and would blow your head off if you were stupid enough to stand in front of the cannon's mouth. Legend has it that Peter's head emerged over the gun shield of Number one gun just as it fired causing Peter to gallop off along the front of the line of guns getting quicker and quicker as each gun went off.

There was an immense pool of horsy knowledge in the King's Troop during those National Service years. Many, maybe as many as 80% of the intake were working with horses before call up and brought with them a great experience in riding stable management and equine care. Some had been called from their employment in hunt stables. Others were apprentice jockeys, riding school employees, saddlers, taylor's and so on. Most went back to their former employment upon demobilization and much as there was great comradeship and fun amongst the rank and file we were all looking forward to our return to civilian life. Many soldiers would make up a chart with a calendar with days ticked off as their 'Demob Day' approached. It was not unusual to see a soldier immediately upon waking as reveille sounded, reach for a pen and cross off another day towards their release.

During the day our call to various duties was sounded by either trumpet or bugle. Reveille, Parades and Watering Order, were all sounded by trumpet while Last Post and the 'Half Battery Charge' was sounded by bugle. It was one of the most stirring moments at the Royal Tournament in Earls Court when the Musical Drive was called into action by bugle and trumpet. The Last Post was always sounded at 6pm each night as the regimental flag was lowered and greeted with huge respect. Any soldier finding himself caught outside the accommodation would immediately have to halt and stand to attention for the full sounding.

Life was never monotonous and we were kept busy from dawn to dusk. At least once a week we had to work through the night on either prowler guard or stable duty. The year was broken up with displays at agricultural shows throughout the country. The transport of guns, horses and staff from St John's Wood to such shows as the 'Bath and West' or the 'Great Yorkshire Show' was a major operation requiring advance parties to set up temporary stabling and accommodation under canvas or rear parties to take everything down again. I remember that we were always in a constant state of exhaustion and took every opportunity to get our heads down to snatch whatever sleep we could before being called out again.

Full rehearsals took place on a large parkland area on Wormwood Scrubs within sight of the prison. On these occasions I would act as a 'Marker' which meant along with seven other markers we would march into position with a lance and stand smartly to attention with the upright lance held at arm's length to designate the size of the arena. The guns thundered by often clipping the lance with the gun hubcaps. Our instructions were to stand fast unless in fear of being struck by the guns in which case we were to smartly take one step back. With young horses in training it was not unusual to contravene orders by (not smartly) taking several steps to avoid death.

26

In the event of the guns passing the marker so close as he might be struck by the passing wheels he should withdraw his arm holding the lance in a smart and disciplined manner. In the unlikely event of the guns swinging due to the soft ground then in order to prevent injury the marker should take one step back also in a smart and disciplined manner.

Smaller rehearsals for the musical ride took place on a frequent basis on a cinders car park in Regents Park not far from the Barracks. This gave us an opportunity to try young horses and upcoming replacement 'Drivers' in the gun team. The term 'Driver' would be more accurately described as a Postilion, (One who rides the guide horse of a pair).

The Lead driver was normally a Bombardier whose job was to set the pace and direction of the gun carriage, while the Wheel Driver's job was to ensure that the rear two horses in the team could act as a brake where necessary. The middle two horses were controlled by the Centre Driver whose job was not only to ensure that the traces remained taught by ensuring all horses were pulling evenly but to keep the shape of the team on the turns and circles. A slack trace would allow a team horse to get a leg over the trace and resulted in stopping the whole ride while the traces were sorted out. (Hence, 'Kicking over the traces.')

With all the above points in mind a pageant of galloping, circling, counter-circling ride of 36 horses pulling six guns and limbers had been devised. The highlight of the year was three weeks at the Earls Court Arena to take part in the Royal Tournament. This was an unashamed display of the Armed Services showing off their respective attractions as a massive recruiting drive and fund raiser for Armed Forces charities. Our part of the display was to perform two rides a day six days a week, (matinee and evening performances). Being under cover and indoors, the horses would gallop out of the arena in huge clouds of steam as though they had just completed the Grand National.

The care of horses was paramount and first class. All horses were gently walked until dried off while hitherto immaculately polished harness was washed off and prepared for the next ride. Every morning would see the same horses being gently led round the car park to ease off cramped muscles from the night before. It was always touching to see personnel from the Royal Navy and Fleet Air Arm volunteering to lead our horses round for twenty minutes while we got on with mucking out and setting the temporary stables fair.

Before each display the gun teams were inspected and marked for the turnout of guns and teams. At the end of the three weeks a winning team would be awarded the honour of 'Silver Stick' whereby each of the three drivers received an engraved riding stock.

By March of 1959 I graduated to Centre Driver and went on several rehearsals before the RSM (Regimental Sergeant Major Dove) rode up and said, 'Petter, aren't you due for demob in August?'

'That's right Sir.' I replied cheerfully whilst at the same time mentally reviewing my demob chart. "Only five months to do."

'Well unless you are prepared to sign on as a regular soldier we will have to find someone else for 'C Sub Centre Driver.''

I remember him laughing as I pointed out I had a job waiting which paid double money for half the hours I was working in the Army and that whilst I appreciated his kind invitation to 'Sign On,' I must decline his thoughtful offer.

So in August 1959 I left the King's Troop Royal Horse Artillery having never fired a shot in anger to join The Metropolitan Police.

Looking back I realize that it could be compared to a finishing school following my six years at the Grammar School and a brief spell in the Police Cadets. We were toughened up, super fit, and accomplished horsemen who had learnt pride in our Regiment.

It was to be some 15 years later that I rode into the barracks at St John's Wood as an Inspector. I was invited into The Officers' Mess for lunch, I think they wanted some variety over their meal as they asked about mounted police work, purchase and training of the police horse and the like. They couldn't have been more supportive or encouraging and it caused much merriment when I revealed that I used to be a Squaddy in 'C' subsection.

Chapter Eight
The Trains Coming

As I mentioned earlier, The King's Troop was blessed with the most talented riding masters that one could find. In Ben Jones and Eric Witts we couldn't have found better instructors. Ben was a hard knowledgeable man, great disciplinarian who went on to win an Olympic gold medal in the three-day event in Mexico in 1968. In the summer evenings Ben would grab any available squaddy to help him build a cross-country course on some derelict bombed out property adjacent to the barracks. The rewards were that we could all have a crack at it. With the workload of the Musical Ride and daily rough exercise, all the horses were extremely fit and loved to get the chance of a cross-country jump.

Eric Witts was a similarly talented instructor who returned to racehorse training when he retired from the Army. He was more refined and in keeping with a civilian riding instructor. Not so harsh as Ben but still got good results.

The troop was an all male environment. The pay was abysmal. 24 shillings, (1 Euro) a week upon joining and only three pounds ten shillings (3 Euro)after eighteen months, with two Rail Travel Vouchers a year to get home. Some of the lads lived as far afield as Scotland and Ireland and could never afford a fare home without the vouchers. I was lucky in so much as I only lived about two hours away by rail and could get home and back on a 48-hour pass. Telephones were a rare commodity and even if you could use the one in the Guard House there was no one to phone as the general public were yet to be connected.

With only a pittance for pay and little time off, the refined young ladies of St John's Wood and Swiss Cottage were rarely tempted to strike up a relationship with Gunners of the King's Troop. They would happily smile and respond to whistles as the soldiers passed either on rough exercise or with full regalia riding down to Hyde Park for a Royal Salute, but I wasn't aware of any great success by any of the troop getting lucky.

Of course there was the occasional camp follower to which some succumbed but for health reasons generally avoided by most. Looking back over 50 years and judging by today's standards, it's amazing to think that young men in their late teens remained mainly celibate for the most part of two years.

The next two years passed in a haze of parades, Royal Salutes, three weeks each year at the Royal Tournament in Earls Court and a succession of advance and rear parties at various agricultural shows around the country. The only respite came every summer when we would spend a few days camped out on the moors with our horses at what was referred to as Summer Camp. We would swim rivers with our horses, slipping off their backs as they rolled on their sides and grabbing their tail in true wild west fashion, there were intersubsection competitions, making our own cross country course, field kitchens and great fun for two or three days.

Something I'll always remember about summer camp was the day our section Sergeant, Sergeant Coward, normally a strict but very fair disciplinarian made the mistake of putting me in charge of map reading in a small detachment tasked with making a twenty mile journey across the Yorkshire moors. He made this decision on the basis that I was the only one with 'O' level GCE in Geography and as such must be pretty hot on ordnance survey, something with which I had to modestly agree.

My academic superiority cut little ice with my newly appointed team however but they reluctantly accepted that I was the only one who knew where we were going. One of our four-man team was a soldier called Glasby, a Yorkshire man of dour wit and a bit of attitude who didn't necessarily respect my new found status in being team leader. Indeed, nor did the other team members.

However my credibility rose when we were the first team to arrive at first map reference well ahead of the rest of the teams. It was short-lived credibility however and Gunner Glasby was to emerge as our hero of the day.

It was quite apparent that grid references on ordnance survey maps meant nothing to the rest of the team and having led them successfully to our first point and after studying the map, they accepted my explanation that the next point of call which was five miles away by the designated route, could be reduced to only two miles if we jumped over a stile into a conservation area and forded a river. Such a plan would ensure our arrival at the next point a good 40 minutes before anyone else.

There was myself on "Go anywhere Peter," Glasby and Johny Wade on horses whose names I can't remember and a new young ex-racing lad whose name I also can't remember riding "Round as a little apple Noggin." Now as I said earlier, "Peter," would go anywhere, whether under the control of a rider or not. He would jump any thing and had he been pulling guns in the First World War would have won a medal for gallantry. The other three riders were all ex-racing lads and better or more experienced riders than me. 'Noggin' however, although everyone's favourite on rough exercise because of her "round as a little apple" shape and therefore the most comfortable under a blanket, was absolutely hopeless on any riding school activity. Jumping anything was definitely not her scene; indeed she was able to execute a right angle turn at a flat out gallop if confronted by anything that needed her to lift her front legs. Nevertheless I felt that if the three of us jumped into the conservation area first and rode on for a bit, we stood a good chance of "Noggin" joining us because of her inbred herding instinct. If my plan failed we could always jump back out again and take the long route.

I led the way on "Go anywhere Peter" and the other two followed in fine style cantering on for about 50 yards before turning to watch in astonishment as "Noggin" sailed over the fence to join us without turning a hair. 'Fookin hell,' said Glasby with Johny Wade nodding in sage agreement. I could feel my credibility growing by the minute.

We rode on for about a mile, following the vaguely marked path that ran alongside a single-track railway line down to the river. The sun was on our backs and we were miles ahead of anyone else and soon picked up the sound of running water. Only it wasn't running it was rushing and we stood in dismay looking down a steep bank onto a fairly wide, deep and fast flowing river. I could feel my credibility rapidly slipping away as the team realized we would have to retrace our steps and lose our advantage.

It was at this moment I heard a train whistle and the clatter of wheels on the railway line, which was about 50 feet above us as it crossed a viaduct over the river. 'Wait a Minute,' I said as I examined the map again, sure enough the railway line went in exactly the right direction. It was a simple iron bridge with solid iron suspension girders arching over it for support. I could see the doubt in their eyes as I suggested we rode up the bank to at least take a look and see if there was a path alongside the track and over the bridge.

It was a bit of a scramble to clamber up the bank but our efforts were rewarded by seeing a footplate bridge of wooden planks running alongside the line for about eighty yards to the other side of the river. It was a single-track line and we surveyed the scene in silence for a while, 'There might be a train coming.' said somebody. The thought of a train bearing down on us as we crossed the narrow footbridge was horrifying. 'The train has only just passed' I said, 'It will only take a minute to walk over if we get off and lead them.' 'There might be a train coming from the other direction,' said another. 'Let's do it if we are going to, before the next train.' I said, rapidly dismounting and running up the stirrup irons. "I'll go first with Peter, he won't baulk, and faint hearted Noggin can bring up the rear if we give her a lead."

Although we could see the river below us through the boardwalk it was easy, 'Peter' came along like a dream and the others followed with words of encouragement to each other and to our horses. We made rapid progress and there was no sign of a train coming. I was almost off the bridge when there was a loud clang and the whole bridge resounded and reverberated. It seemed as though it had been hit with a sledgehammer. There was a terrific clatter coming from behind me together with a frantic cry for help from Noggin's rider. I looked back as I left the bridge and broke into a cold sweat as I saw Noggin down on her chest with a leg straddled either side of a rail. God help us if a train should come at this moment.

By now both Johny Wade and Glasby were off the bridge. "Don't leave me" yelled Noggin's rider as he desperately tried to lift her off the rail. "Quick Johny, ride along the track and flag down the train if it's coming." Just off the bridge was a five-barred gate leading into a meadow. "We'll turn our horses into the field and go back for Noggin."

Johny saw no point in arguing that the train was just as likely to come from behind us, he could see that at least we could increase our chances of avoiding disaster by half as he cantered off to flag the train down in true wild-west style should one be coming. I grabbed Glasby's horse and together with mine led them into the meadow. It was at this point that Glasby showed true strength and courage. He ran back to the fallen horse and to this day I don't know how he did it, but, clasping both hands around one of Noggin's front legs gave a heave and she was up and only too happy to charge off the bridge to join the others.

Noggin had sustained some grazes to the underside of her belly and on the inside of her front legs but otherwise was none the worse for the incident. All thought of arriving first at our destination disappeared as we gratefully turned the horses loose to graze while we all had a cigarette and generally agreed that I was mad to have suggested such a thing.

My credibility had taken a downturn, but in the manner of true British Squaddies we soon laughed it off as we heard the train approaching. We thanked our lucky stars that we had escaped quickly enough to avoid poor Noggin being sliced in two. It seems that as we were crossing the bridge Noggin had kicked a side stanchion causing the metal work to rattle and ring like a bell.

Finally on the 8th August 1959 I was demobilized. Remarkably fit and with the best possible knowledge on horse care and equitation and was more than ready to return to the Police Service. With previous experience as a Police Cadet the re-entry into the Met Police was a formality and on the 7th September I reported to Peel House to be sworn in as Constable.

Chapter Nine

On The Beat In Stoke Newington

Looking back, I suppose the Police Force as we all called it in those days was poorly paid and not a very popular calling. The establishment was set at 20000 personnel, with virtually no civilian support and no traffic wardens. Officers were leaving for better pay and our current strength was only about 13000.

For me however it was a "life's ambition come true." Although I had completed two years Military Service with the Royal Horse Artillery and thought I might eventually apply for Mounted Branch my main thoughts were just to enjoy the training and get out on the streets of London and see what life held in store for me.

I was about to embark upon the most enjoyable period of my life. The comradeship, catching criminals, meeting the public, dealing with people's social problems, traffic accident enquiries, summonses, going to court, policing public order events and large crowds at football matches such as the Arsenal Football club at Highbury, were to become my way of life for the next three years and one which gave me great satisfaction and purpose.

The initial training course of 13 weeks was residential but unlike the Army we could get home for the weekends. The pay was more than double than I had been getting and life was good, albeit crammed with masses of information on law and procedures to equip us for the outside world. There were many practical exercises, all conducted by well-informed instructors, all involving much humour but with an underlying purpose which would get the intended message across. The daily courses were reinforced by evening study where we learnt line and verse off by heart. Written tests the following day would ensure that we were up to speed.

So in December 1959 we anxiously scanned the notices to find our new station. With suitcases packed with uniform we joined the Force coach and set off from Victoria to what seemed like every possible police station in London. It was just my luck to be posted to Stoke Newington in North London, the very last drop off point. We painfully made our way through South and West London before finally being dropped off in Stoke Newington High Street some three hours later.

Upon reporting to the Sergeant in the front office we were promptly directed to the Chief Superintendent's Clerks who ushered us into the great man's presence for a formal welcome. "This will only take a couple of minutes" he said brightly. This 'couple of minutes,' turned out to be nearly an hour. Unfortunately we were still wearing greatcoats and the Chief Superintendent had the heating on at full blast. It must have been his way of testing our endurance because we were kept standing for the whole interview and near to passing out when we were finally released.

However having passed our endurance test we were shown to our new quarters where I was to reside for the next three years. Stoke Newington Police Section House for single, (all male) officers was an unimposing old Victorian accommodation on three floors with 50 individual rooms. On the ground floor were two canteens, a small lounge with, wonder of wonders, a black and white TV and a kitchen. There were two canteens, one for non-residents and one exclusively for residents.

It was in this small lounge that I experienced my first example of racial prejudice within the force. While I tinkered with the brand new black and white TV trying to get some sort of a picture a young Scottish Police Constable came in having just finished his early morning shift at Kings Cross. We very quickly got talking and once he learnt that I was fresh out of Training School took it upon himself to lecture me on how to forget my Training School experiences and realize that I was now in the real world. It transpired that he had already been a fully-fledged Constable for two years or more and in his heavy Scottish brogue he commenced to explain to me how I should conduct myself for the future.

In his eyes I was about to embark on a world filled with the most evil people bent on crime with murderous intent particularly towards the Police. The most evil being the recently arrived West Indian Community which was settling into North London in their Thousands. None of whom could be trusted, all on drugs and carrying knives.

I had always been positive and optimistic by nature and responded by saying they can't all be bad, that the majority were surely looking for a decent way of life. His whole attitude changed as making frequent use of the 'N' word he directed his hatred towards me for being what he referred to as naive and a "Nigger Lover."

It transpired that he had never known any other way of life since leaving school other than the Police and I took no time in telling him so, "You need a spell in the Army son and realize what it's like for the rest of the world."

I still remember his sneering reply when he said (as though it were the most outrageous thing imaginable) "I suppose that you are one of these 'Do Gooders' who call the blacks, Sir, don't you?" My response of, "If it's appropriate, I would" prompted him to leave the lounge in disgust.

I was mature enough to realize that although there was some prejudice, his attitude was not the norm and that his extremism would catch him out eventually.

Not that the West Indian Community in North London didn't create tension. Since the arrival of the early West Indian Immigrants some ten years earlier, there had been a gradual build up of population with insufficient housing to accommodate them. This fact and a completely different culture of music and all night partying became the bane of the 'Beat Bobby's' life as he strove to deal with the complaints from residents. Compelled to live with reggae being blasted out on massive loud speakers for a whole weekend with only a short break of a couple of hours before it would start again drove the neighbours to despair as they tried to lead the quiet life that they had previously enjoyed. Large groups would spill out onto the pavement and roads on a summer night and with little or no toilet arrangements neighbour's gardens were the normal relief as they sought some place to go. There were complaints of illicit sales of alcohol and use of banned drugs, knife carrying and incessant rowdyism.

We would respond to complaints by asking for the occupier to turn down the music or turn it off completely if it was late. Such people were normally polite and co-operative and would immediately comply only for it to be put straight back up to full volume as soon as we left. Such behaviour eventually resulted in the local Superintendent arranging for a raid on the most troublesome premises while evidence for sale of alcohol, possession of drugs and offensive weapons was gathered and arrests made.

It was on my first such raid that although our patience was tried to the hilt we couldn't help but see the funny side of their complaints that we were denying them a good time based on the right to illegal booze, cannabis, street fights and reggae. Not that other nationalities were going to be outdone of having a good time of booze, music and fights, it's just that they mainly did so on licensed premises during licensing hours or shortly after without high volume amplifiers.

The next three years were to become the happiest time of my life. Stoke Newington was a wonderful ground for a young Policeman to gain experience. In the early Sixties there was a high crime rate of theft from all types of premises from private houses to business premises. The Kray twins were at their most active with extortion and violence.

The biggest thrill was to make a good arrest for crime, these were the times when the patrolling Police Officer would parade for duty and then patrol on his own on a set beat for his eight hour shift returning to the station only once for a forty five minute refreshment break unless he made an arrest or had reports to complete. We had no vehicles or radio contact with the station could only be made through a 'Police Box or Police Post system', no stab proof clothing and just a wooden truncheon for self defence.

It was a time when many or most of our constables were ex servicemen who had seen active service during the war or had all completed National Service for two years in one of the Armed Services. Consequently most of the force were very smart and presented a very good image when they stepped out on the streets. The old Dickensian style high collar had disappeared and replaced with a smart detachable collar and tie. Light wet weather would see a constable patrolling in a cape while a heavy raincoat or greatcoat was worn for bad weather.

These were 'heady' days for young single police constables. Section House life was a great medium for forging new friendships and socializing. We were all very keen and it was here I was to meet a lifelong friend Ron Chapman who was so determined to get into the C.I.D. that he would go out in his aged Standard Ten and sit on observations while he waited for guys wanted on warrant to emerge and make an off duty arrest. He had been very well trained by his father in vehicle maintenance and home decoration and when I first met him he was performing a de-coke and re-bore on the engine. I cheerfully set to grinding valves and fitting new piston rings under his supervision and agreed to go out with him while he conducted these off duty surveillances. Though we both followed different careers we both went on to take promotion and stood as best man for each other's weddings and assisted each other in decorating our first houses.

Ron went on to complete a distinguished career in the C.I.D where as Detective Superintendent he headed the Crime Squad for North East London.

During the winters of the late 50's early 60's terrible smogs would descend over London and the ghostly appearance of a constable in helmet and cape was a sight reminiscent of the days of 'Jack the Ripper'.

We would parade for duty at the start of our eight-hour shifts, where the Sergeant would read out relevant information affecting the crime scene in London that the station had received by teleprinter from other stations, Scotland Yard, or published information regarding wanted or missing persons. We would make notes and be supplied with request for visits to various addresses on our beat to gather statements and information as requested from other stations.

The whole parade would be concluded by a visit from the Duty Officer or overall shift supervisor who was of Inspector rank. He would then give a brief pep talk before going through the ceremony of calling "Appointments." To which we would all produce truncheon, whistle and chain and marking materials. The days of marching out to our various beats in column were long gone and we were left to make our own way to commence patrol on our allocated beat for the shift.

With visits to the public for enquiries, regular calls via the police box to the station at set times, and dealing with whatever we encountered on patrol the shifts were full of variety and interest. The eight hours would be split by one forty five minute refreshment break which we would normally take back at the station canteen during which we might be called out to an emergency. At such times we would normally pile into the only station van and head off to wherever needed.

Beat supervision was completed by a patrolling supervising Sergeant and sometimes the patrolling Inspector who would know who should be on which beat. 15 minutes before the end of our shifts we would report to the duty Sergeant who would take our pocket book, accident reports, and summonses issued during our patrol.

Generally speaking the young Constables reports were of a better quality than the seasoned copper who may have fallen into sloppy habits. Nevertheless the Sergeants were always helpful and did their best to make sure our reports would stand up in court or contain the relevant information.

Chapter Ten

Sudden Death

There were a lot of elderly people living alone in private bed-sit flats and it was not unusual to be called to such premises by a concerned neighbour or delivery man who had noticed a build up of delivered milk bottles or papers.

It was on one such occasion that I was called to a ground floor flat in a decaying Victorian building on a bitterly cold foggy November morning. The milkman reported that he had seen no sign of the resident an elderly Jewish lady for a few days and the milk hadn't been taken in. There was no response to my banging on a very solid door which was obviously bolted top and bottom on the inside. Being a ground floor flat it had a rear window overlooking the garden, so making my way round the side of the house I thought it would be a relatively simple task to look in the back window. Unfortunately the style of houses in those days meant that it had a cellar with a stairwell leading to the basement. The window was heavily frosted on the inside and for me to get close enough to peer through the ground floor window I would need to stand at garden level but above the stairwell and stretch across the void with my hands on the window ledge. This manouvre would enable me to bring my face close enough to the window to peer through the grimy frost to the inside. How I would revert to the upright position once I completed my observation without falling into the basement area didn't cross my mind. I suppose I considered myself sufficiently fit enough to spring back using my super strong arms to push off the window ledge.

Having achieved the first part of the exercise my face was now close to the lowest window pane, my exertions had started to produce clouds of steam making the window even more frosted. I managed to make out the dim interior of a large living room. Some distance away and closer to the solid door than to the window was a large leather wing backed chair on which I could make out the outline of a heavily overweight old lady sitting upright with a heavy shawl or blanket round her shoulders. Her head was slightly tilted to the side though she appeared to be staring at me. Balancing on one super strong arm I managed to rap on the window with my free hand. There was no response as she kept staring at me.

"Any sign of her." I nearly fell into the basement area with shock as I realized the milkman had followed me round. "Yes" I answered as casually as I could, "she's a goner I think, a bit spooky, she's sitting up and looking at me."

"Oh God" he said brightly, "how are you going to get back?" "Not a problem" I said casually as I lightly shoved back off the window ledge. Now normally this athletic spring would guarantee my safe return to the vertical position, however I had failed to take into account the fact that I was wearing a heavy greatcoat, which so restricted my athletic spring that I hardly reached halfway. I found myself tilting into the abyss and there was nothing for it but to drop into the cellar well, a good seven foot drop. To my astonishment the resulting leap resulted in me landing with feet together and a crouch which would have done credit to an Olympic gymnast. Making my way up the concrete stairs I turned to the admiring milkman and said, "There now, that wasn't so difficult, was it?" Service pride and dignity had been maintained.

I was pretty confident that the lady had died in the chair but I couldn't be sure. There were no radios or phones in those days and the nearest phone box was 10 minute's walk away. It was vital to get in as quickly as possible. A solid kick sprung the lower bolt while a shoulder charge smashed the door open. If the lady was asleep she certainly had a rude awakening.

Within, it was icy cold, no fire or form of heat. Approaching the back of the chair I could make out the grey wispy hair on the top of her head and her arm resting on the armrest. Reaching down and touching her arm, I noticed it was rock solid and freezing cold. 'You alright love' I called out unnecessarily, the milkman was right on my shoulder as we saw the half consumed bottle of brandy and an empty tablet bottle. At least she had died with some comfort. A quick look round revealed several prepared sealed letters to her friends and family; she had hastened her own death and as such was a suicide.

I needed to secure the letters for the Coroner's inquest and I also needed to arrange for a visit by the Coroner's Officer. None of the letters had any address; just first names but one had a telephone number on it. Thanking the milkman and collecting the letters I secured the premises as best as I could and set off for the nearest telephone.

With the Station Officer informed I was back at the flat within 30 minutes. As I walked in I sensed something had changed. I could no longer see her hair over the back of the chair. As I walked around her I found her head slumped forward and vomit down the front of her chest. 'That's not unusual.' I jumped as the Coroner's Officer came in, "Did you touch her?" "Yes I did, I shook her arm." "That'll be it then," he breezed, "Build up of gas over several days, good job she didn't throw up as you shook her or you might have jumped."

Laughing he arranged for the body to be taken to the Morgue while I awaited the arrival of one of the relatives to secure the property. Within a short time a distressed gentleman who turned out to be the deceased lady's brother together with his wife arrived. While his wife rummaged through the wardrobes I explained to the brother the situation and that there might be a Coroner's Inquest before the body was released. In those days suicide was a crime albeit the only crime you would always get away with if you were successful.

"Where's her ring she had a very valuable diamond ring?" demanded the rummaging sister in law. "The lady had no jewelry on her as far as I could see," I answered, "But she has left some letters addressed to various people which I have secured for the possible inquest." The Brother was silently crying as he accepted the loss of his sister and hushed his wife's strident tones while I said goodbye and returned to the station to make out my report.

It subsequently transpired at the inquest that she had taken her own life while the balance of her mind was disturbed, and that suicide notes were in the letters together with the missing ring and other valuables.

In those days with little or no social services it was quite common to be called to "Sudden Death Incidents" often in very intriguing circumstances. I was on the patrolling Area Car one morning when we were called to a flat in which we found an elderly lady dead on the bathroom floor the cause of death was gas poisoning from an unlit gas jet in the kitchen. We found it odd that her very much alive budgie was chirping merrily in his cage in the lounge, which was situated between the kitchen and the bathroom. The gas must have made its way into the lounge before entering the bathroom, how could the budgie have survived? It transpired that the waves of gas did not reach the budgie's cage in the window before it invaded the bathroom. The prepaid gas meter then ran out before it could reach the window. The caretaker undertook to care for the lucky and very hungry budgie.

There were elderly people dying on buses with heart attacks or collapsing in the street, though I was never called to a murder and although I dealt with some horrible accidents in which young children were injured I was fortunate never to have been involved in a fatal road accident.

Court attendance was a regular part of our life, Magistrates Court, Central Criminal Court sometimes at the 'Old Bailey' and occasional Coroner's Court became part of our normal routine. Most of our time in court would be as a result of traffic summonses that we had prosecuted (no traffic wardens in those days) but quite often we would be involved in crime arrest. These cases would be presented by the Criminal Investigation Department with ourselves called as witnesses.

Night duty was a different world to daylight patrols. Looking back I realize that our system of policing was basically the same that it had been since the force was formed in the nineteenth century. Having been paraded for duty and briefed we would work our beat on foot, paying attention to any known places of rowdyism, vandalism or disorder.

However once the streets became quiet we would arrange our lonely patrol to concentrate on what we thought would be the likeliest places for any thieves to be about. I found that shop premises were always a favourite for a quick smash and grab or a breaking.

On several occasions I would get lucky while standing in the shadows or shop doorways to witness and arrest people carrying their loot away from a shop that they had forced open in the early hours of the morning. Few had cars and would carry their swag. One early morning, together with a colleague we even arrested a guy who had committed a smash and grab on a gent's outfitters on his bicycle. He was riding without lights and seemed to have a bundle of clothes draped over his handlebars and crossbar so I stepped out to stop him. To my astonishment he just put his head down and pedalled like a man possessed. As we ran after him my colleague gave him a push and as he went sprawling in the road I went flying over his fallen bike and by pure chance grabbed the skinniest ankle as he tried to flee.

The sight of the darkened street, the bike, two off-the-peg suits and one beautiful gent's raincoat were only surpassed by three beautiful trilby hats stuffed in the saddle bag complete with the Dunn's price tags attached filled us with delight as we realized we had nabbed a shop breaker.

It transpired that the robber had done Dunn's, the hat shop and even still had the piece of piping in his bag with which he had smashed the window.

Such random stops reaped a surprising success rate in preventing crime or detecting crime if crime was committed. The stops were always recorded not only in the officer's pocket book but in the 'Stop Book' retained at station. This not only protected the officer in the event of a complaint but was also a useful tool in which other officers could see who was out and about on the ground. Legitimate stop and search was encouraged and had the goodwill of the public with whom we would always explain the thinking behind 'stop and search'.

Sometimes you could randomly stop a car in the early hours and find you had stopped a celebrity. On one occasion with about two week's service I stopped a luxurious Jaguar in Upper Clapton. Young and inexperienced I found the gentleman to be extremely polite and understanding. He insisted I searched the boot, glove compartment and pockets of the car. He even volunteered to lift the bonnet and empty his pockets. He couldn't have been more accommodating.

I dutifully recorded his details as I inspected his licence and wished him goodnight. I thought it odd as he shook my hand and asked to be remembered to all the officers back at the station and sped off in the direction of Bethnal Green. Back at the station I transferred his details into the stop book and then went to the canteen for refreshments when a voice called out my divisional number. "Who's One Forty Four?"

"That's me." I replied looking up to see Police Constable Kirby with the stop book in his hand and the duty Sergeant looking over his shoulder.

'You've just stopped Ronnie Kray, do you know who he is?'

I couldn't understand the hilarity caused by my innocent "No I don't but he sends his regards to the station," until it was explained that the Kray Twins were the most notorious gangsters in London.

On one occasion at about 2am while having a crafty smoke behind a street hoarding I was astonished to see a young couple emerge from the alley at the back of a row of shops carrying a suitcase that was so heavy he had to keep putting it down on the road every few steps. His female accomplice turned out to be heavily pregnant and their furtive manner wouldn't have been out of place on the stage if it wasn't for the fact it was real.

They must have been about fifty yards away and as they disappeared into a side street across the road. I quickly emerged from my shadowy hide and ran after them only to be further astonished to see another human shape emerge from the same alley with another heavy suitcase.

Unfortunately by then I was in full flight and he saw me from about thirty yards. I had to give him credit for effort and tenacity for hanging on to the suitcase as he accelerated into the same side street.

I thought I was fairly fit and able to shift a bit perhaps my greatcoat and heavy boots held me back but as I rounded the corner into the dimly lit side street there was no one, not a soul, the street was empty.

Two grown men a heavily pregnant lady and two large heavy suitcases....gone... gone in about three seconds.

Drawing my truncheon I started to check the premises. The first being a garden with a low, two foot high wall at the back. In the gloom I could make out the outline of three heads as they crouched behind the wall. This was real Keystone Cops stuff but I reasoned that they would not be looking for violence considering the presence of the expectant mother.

One mustn't forget that in those days we had no radio or mobile phone only a truncheon and a whistle and chain, (Oh, and appointments). So there was nothing for it but to bluff it out with, 'OK lads, the games up, come on out.' The two men stepped forward while the expectant mother kept her head down and stayed put, doing her best to hide behind the parapet. 'And bring the cases with you' I said, feigning ignorance of the third person.

They sheepishly went back for the suitcases while I wondered what sort of thieves were these, running around at the dead of night, loaded down with booty accompanied by a mother to be. Surely it must be a moonlight flit.

"What's in the suitcases?" "Books, pots and PANS, food," came the answer. "Where are you going?" "We live here."

"What's in the lady's bag"? With a sigh of relief the lady stood up from her cramped position. "Baby Clothes." She called out in a clear voice.

"Open the cases." "We can't, they belong to a friend and he's got the key."' It was a dream of a catch if I could only get them back to the station. There was no point in further questioning until I could do so. "Do you live here lady?"' "I do." "Got the key?" "Yes, and that's my husband and brother."

"OK, go inside turn the light on so that I can see it's your place and I'll take these two to the station."

And that was it, as the two men walked in front of me I heard them muttering about making a run for it or having a go at me but they had enough savvy to realize there was their accomplice in the house. I must confess that I left them in no uncertain terms regarding my action if they tried anything. And so they quietly walked the two hundred yards to the police post carrying the suitcases where I was able to call for assistance and transport.

Once at the station it was a delight to see the cases were packed full of brand new transistor radios which they had just stolen from a shop display by removing the bricks from the back wall of a radio and TV shop.

The CID were quickly on the scene and after a quick chat with me hounded off to the gangs residence and soon returned with the young mother to be and her bag of, not baby clothes but, (you've guessed it) transistor radios.

During our two-year probation we would be attached for two weeks at a time to different departments for experience. Such departments would be CID or Traffic Patrol and the like.

One department not on offer for short term attachment was the Mounted Branch, not only because it was impractical but also for health and safety reasons. Many stations throughout the Met had small stable attachments, some with as few as only three horses. For the most part the stables consisted of six horses and Stoke Newington was no exception. My desire to join the Mounted Branch was waning a little as I got caught up in the enjoyment of day-to-day policing. Nevertheless I kept my hand in with horses by making regular visits to the stables and riding whenever I got the chance on my trips back home to Sussex.

It was a wonderful time, a wonderful ground for a young police officer to work. There was great comradeship and some hilariously funny moments. The social scene was great fun with frequent invitations from the nurses to the local hospital dances. Many a police officer and nurse found themselves walking down the aisle following these liaisons and it was here that I was to meet Christine who was to become my lovely wife and mother of our two lovely children.

Looking back I must confess that it was with much soul searching before I applied to join the Mounted Branch. I loved the life on the beat but accepted that the previous effort I had applied through my service in the King's Troop would be a complete waste if I didn't follow it through and transfer.

I was promptly turned down on my first application and although I was invited to apply again was more than happy to continue with my foot duty role at Stoke Newington.

Chapter Eleven
Picador and Badminton

Picture by kind permission of Clive Hiles. Equestrian Photographer.

**Picador was a bit surprised by the drop
in this Intermediate Event**

After serving for three wonderful year's ordinary foot duty at Stoke Newington I received a call from the Mounted Branch administrative office to reapply for selection. Training courses ran every six months and invitations to apply were regularly posted in Police Orders. I hadn't bothered to respond due to the fact I was to be married during the course. My new wife and I were looking forward to two weeks honeymoon in Jersey and I had no intention of re-arranging our wedding day. The Mounted Chief Superintendent, Harry Griffin, sent a message to say that in view of my previous experience with the King's Troop I could attend a shortened course which would overcome the problem.

Consequently it was October 1962 that I joined the Mounted Branch at Imber Court and subsequently posted to the stables in Stoke Newington in 1963.

All seasoned Mounted Police Officers can recall particular horses that were a nightmare on certain occasions. There was an element of pride in overcoming each horse's difficulties rather than give up in defeat. I have seen some situations where officers were losing sleep or close to nervous breakdown when on a daily basis were constantly faced with the plight of negotiating their respective mounts imagined horrors and fears in London's traffic.

My first allocated horse was such a reject; he was everything a police horse shouldn't be. Rather than admit defeat his previous rider had emigrated to Australia with his family to escape his dilemma. I first became aware of my new mount whilst serving my initial strapping period at Stoke Newington stables back in 1963. I received a phone call from 'Jock Gillespie' my Chief Inspector. 'Ayeee, Petter,' he started with his strong Scottish brogue. 'I'm transferring you to Hackney, it'll be closer to home and there's a horse waiting for you called Mark. He's not been out for long, he's had some problems but the vacancy has come about through his riders leaving for Australia, you should be able to sort him out.'

'Sort him out,' 'regular rider heading for Australia', he couldn't have put more distance between himself and the horse short of going to the moon. But with the confidence of youth I happily moved my uniform to the five-horse stable attached to Hackney Police Station in Mare Street to make my acquaintance with Police Horse 'Mark.'

Mark was a five-year old grey cob. 15.2 hands, fat, hog-maned, flat eared on approach, tail swishing, mean looking and showing signs of hatred for the human race. Using a lifetime of equine skills

I was able to sidle up between him and the stall wall. I spoke in soothing tones and stroked his neck as he somehow managed to flatten his ears even more. He obviously thought it was a trick. 'I've got the answer to you mister,' I thought, as I noticed the now interested gathering of my new stable mates out in the stable aisle. His ears suddenly pricked forward as I reached into my pocket and brought out a packet of Polos. Up to that point I had been holding his stable head collar, which I now felt safe to relax as I unwrapped the first delight. But Mark was no ordinary sweet natured horse who would respond to kindness. Oh no, viciously stamping his front nearside hoof and narrowly missing my foot he lunged at my hands and somehow managed to grab the complete packet and flick my middle finger between his front teeth. There we stood, finger locked in his jaw, Polo packet on the floor and watched with extreme mirth from the aisle by my new stable mates, Sandy Wallace had even stuffed his apron in his mouth to prevent laughing.

Plunging my free hand into his mouth and grabbing his tongue I was able to get him to release my finger while I made good my escape down the side of the stall and past his madly swishing tail. By now my new stable mates were reduced to tears and hysterics while Mark scoffed the whole packet of Polos complete with wrapper.

Over a much needed cup of tea. My new friends filled me with foreboding as they recounted how Mark was even worse on the streets. 'I'll sort him out,' I thought. 'Are there any open spaces nearby where I can give him a spin or a workout?' I asked. 'Hackney Marsh, about a mile away, I'll give you a lead over there if you like,' said Brian Dickinson my new colleague.

So some half hour later we were uniformed and tacked up heading out the back gate of Hackney Police Station into London's traffic. My problems were just beginning. We emerged into the narrow street, cars parked either side, two horses abreast with me on the inside dropping back to single file if we met any moving traffic. Coming towards us and leaving barely enough room for a horse to pass was a dustcart Brian led the way with his black horse Ogden. Mark made it quite clear he was having none of it, use of legs and urges to go forward only met with half rears as he promptly dived between two cars and up onto the pavement where he was able to proceed until he passed the lorry.

Hackney marshes couldn't come soon enough as we headed east across the river Lea. Here I was able to give him some quiet schooling before giving him his head as he joyously galloped along the open spaces.

We returned to the stables in a much more relaxed manner and I felt optimistic for the future. The following days I felt we were getting somewhere as I regularly schooled him and patrolled the streets of Hackney. Whenever we encountered large vehicles we would tuck into a convenient space while the vehicle passed. However if a large vehicle was double-parked he would stubbornly refuse to go forward. Legs, hand and voice were to no avail, even resorting to using a light stick or riding crop made no difference and the only way he could be persuaded to continue with his patrol was to reign backwards until we passed the vehicle. As I had no intention of resigning or emigrating I persevered and accepted his shortcomings. He was good in a crowd and seemed to enjoy State occasions.

On the face of things I shouldn't have been more contented with my lot but the truth was that I felt unfulfilled as a police officer in not being on the ground with day to day police duty. I had enjoyed arresting the villains of Stoke Newington, the court appearances even at London Sessions and the Old Bailey and day to day police duty. This was not the case in Mounted Branch. Sure we did come into contact with the public and we did make arrests for public order offences at football matches. Over my thirty years in the Mounted Branch, Mounted Officers played their part in striking a good rapport with the public, successfully capturing criminals for housebreaking or fleeing from the scene of crime. There were energetic officers who frequently would feature on the charge sheet when they made arrests at football matches for public order offences, Mick Gettens later to become Inspector, who in hot pursuit captured a man subsequently charged with attempted murder.

Sadly there was always the odd officer who was little more than a uniform carrier. It was my experience that the most active officers were immaculate in their turnout and care of horses, who took a pride in their interaction with the public and could be relied upon to patrol unsupervised and keen to be out on the streets.

I remained keen to get involved, dealt with traffic offences, helped the public whilst on patrol, the odd court appearance following disorder in crowd control but somehow, for me anyway, it didn't match the excitement of policing on foot. All this was soon to change.

I was seriously considering going back to ordinary duty when after some six months I received another call from Chief Inspector Jock Gillespie. 'Ayyyyeee Petter' came his educated Scottish accent, 'I want you to take on a different horse that's having problems over at East Ham. He's a fine looking 3 year old and he's come out to duty before he's ready so I'm transferring you to Chigwell near the forest where you can complete his training. I'm passing that horse of yours onto Bernard Barker, he can ride him on The Grey Escort, State visits, 'Opening of Parliament' and the like'. Bernard was ex Household Cavalry and an accomplished horseman. Blunt and to the point he informed me that he would find a way to pass large vehicles without having to reign back. Consequently the following day I said my farewells to Mark with an apple which he furiously grabbed before attempting to stamp on my foot as he climbed on the horsebox for transport to Richmond Park. Bernard successfully used him on a couple of ceremonial events before Mark had to be put down following an incident where he trapped his leg between a car radiator and the front bumper. Meanwhile I collected my new horse from East Ham stables and was off to the leafy suburbs of Chigwell with my new horse Picador.

Picador was everything Mark was not. He had obviously been handled a lot as a foal and was kind by nature, would gently take sugar cubes from your lips with his soft muzzle and snickered a welcome of greeting whenever you first entered the stable. Over 16.2 hands, Irish Draft crossed with thoroughbred and almost black in colour apart from a grey muzzle. As is usual in such markings he

Picador as a three year old. Chigwell c1965

And again three years later when he was "Eventing".

was later to turn a full white, or grey as they say.

He had a shock of a mane that Thelwell would have loved in his cartoons and no attempt to tidy or tame it could bring it under control. In time I had to settle for a hog mane, but he still looked magnificent. I was posted late turn for my first ride on Picador, unlike Mark with his coarse coat Picador had the fine hair of a thoroughbred. I prepared him for our first patrol his coat shone in the bright sun as I headed out through the stable gate for what I thought would be a nice ride through Epping Forest.

Whoops! I'd travelled about 15 yards before he performed a rear that would have not been out of place in The Spanish Riding School. As I leant forward he came down before performing another majestic rear. Now police horses are not supposed to rear and I had no reason to believe that this was a circus act, he just did not want to leave the stable. 'Sit tight Andy' shouted Jock Wallace as he emerged from the tack room with Brian Dickinson. So with one either side they led me out into the back road and pointed me towards the main road. Every time they released the head collar Picador would baulk and stubbornly dig his heels in as I urged him forward. The back road to the main road was about 200 yards long as we made our unsteady zigzag and nap route to set off to serve the public.

He just didn't want to go, whether he had a sore back or had bad memories of West Ham or was just being plain stubborn I couldn't say but persuasion and coaxing got me nowhere. However once I got him into a trot he made some progress albeit with some naps. If I saw a vehicle approaching I would pull into a nearby drive or gap until it passed. I made my unsteady way up Buckhurst Hill and over the river Roding where I dived into the nearest field, jumped off, removed the bit from his mouth and let him graze on the lush grass by the river bank for twenty minutes before heading back towards the stable which he performed without a murmur.

The next day he couldn't leave the stable quickly enough as we headed off for his grazing patch. A changed horse with a completely different attitude to the fears he had felt around East Ham, he was happy to trot along at a strong pace towards the river Roding. I felt him begin to lag as we approached his new found fields, pushing him on at a strong trot we passed the gate and for the next half mile trotted him up the good rise of Buckhurst Hill into the forest where again I promptly let him graze. After that second day and forever afterwards he loved his forest patrols.

It was while serving at Chigwell I was selected for Sergeant. Upon hearing of my selection my good friend Brian Dickinson advised me to join the Freemasons and help my career. I had of course vaguely heard of the Freemasons but it had never appealed to me. Brian explained that it was a secret organization whose members would help one another, that they also financially supported worthy causes, that one was never invited to join and if I was interested he could provide me with the details.

Despite their philanthropic generosity, it struck me as being unfair. I could instantly see the disadvantage to a hopeful at any interview for a post if he didn't know whether or not some advantage existed to benefit the competition. Without any animosity I resolved that it went against my core morality and resolved not to join in the ancient rituals of Freemasonry. This decision never seemed to hold me back as I progressed through the ranks to Chief Inspector.

Then at this rank I lost out to selection for Superintendent. But one can never tell and there lies the rub, I was eventually selected and hold no grudge. I eventually became philanthropic by joining my local Rotary Club which has no secrets.

Life in 1964 couldn't have been better, with my lovely wife Christine of just two year's, we purchased our first house in Hainault, only ten minutes from the stable and a young horse to bring on in the beautiful surrounds of the forest I was in my element.

Chigwell stables were originally part of the old Chigwell Manor and Belmont House before it was purchased as a sports complex and social club for the Metropolitan Police in 1926. Within the grounds was a six- horse stable that used to serve the old house for transport. Having been closed for decades it was decided in 1963 to open the stables for five months of the summer.

Primarily set up for crime prevention in the forest, theft from cars, indecency, flashing and even rape had all been recorded in the crime books of Loughton, Woodford and Waltham Abbey as people had been accosted in the woods. We would patrol from 9am through to 8pm on a shift pattern for seven days a week. As a result of the mounted patrols the entries in the crime books reduced by 90%.

The wonder of it all was we were being paid for riding top quality horses in glorious surroundings. It was ideal country for bringing on young horses and gave Picador and myself an opportunity to complete his training. The forest was heavily wooded with some riding tracks which local riding stables had to adhere to but we were given licence to go off ride in the interest of crime prevention. Consequently there were many ditches and fallen trees to negotiate. Over the next couple of months Picador became relaxed and muscled up into a fine mount who would have been a popular choice on any hunt.

If we came across any road hazards such as pneumatic drills, skip lorries and the like where his courage failed him, a push with the legs into trot seemed to overcome his fears. On one occasion while riding the 8-mile journey into Bow stables to be shod we found ourselves in a strong trot along the dual carriageway that lies between Stratford and Bow. The passing traffic is very fast on this section, it was double lane in each direction with a low dividing wall between the carriageways. The wall was only about eighteen inches high and would never be acceptable by today's standards. It had a nice five-foot wide grass bank down the middle, with a similar wall on the other side. This rather neat barrier was designed to separate the traffic flowing in either direction. I always found it best to trot this one mile section keeping close to the left hand kerb as the traffic whizzed by at about forty miles an hour. On this rainy day about half way along I noticed a high backed articulated lorry illegally parked against the kerb with its warning flashers blinking in the gloom, all traffic had slowed to overtake it and I signalled my intention to do the same. Following drivers had the good sense to give me room to move into the outside lane as I trotted past the

Artic. Half way past the lorry the driver decided to pull away with much revving of engine and hissing of airbrakes. Picador's reaction was spectacular as he hopped up on the wall and onto the grass divide, he cantered beautifully down the centre while the unconcerned lorry driver made good his escape. The drivers behind me were magnificent as they patiently watched this unusual spectacle of equine skill. I had no choice but to direct him back onto the road. His nimbleness was breathtaking as he hopped off the bank back onto the metalled road without a slip and continued his journey to the forge.

In 1964 The Metropolitan Police had 26 stables of varying sizes ranging from just three horses at Plaistow and West Ham to 18 horses or more at Bow, Hammersmith and Great Scotland Yard.

We had no horse transport in those days apart from one immaculate and rarely used three horse box at the training establishment. Consequently because of the long treks to Imber Court all four districts were directed to hold Mounted Drill twice a week at approved locations around London.

Wanstead Flats was allocated as our training ground for the North-East corner of the London where we had authority to train twice a week throughout the summer months. The public would visit and stand at a safe distance while we ran through certain drills as a unit rehearsing single file, double file, line abreast, half passes and other movements to be used on public order under the superb instruction of Chief Inspector Jim Pawley.

This training would then be followed by 'Tent Pegging' with lance, show jumping and 'Sword Lance and Revolver' training as we prepared for the Annual Horse Show in July. Both horse and rider benefited enormously from such exercise and the ride to and from the training ground ensured that the horse remained fit and well down to their work.

Picador loved to get on the soft ground, loved to gallop into the tent pegging runs and was a natural jumper. Winning the Police Show Jumping Classes at Imber Court in his first year confirmed my view that he was something special.

Unfortunately he hated standing on state occasions, or perhaps he loved them and wanted to join in. Either way, the sound of an approaching marching band or the brilliant pageantry of state carriages led by the Household Cavalry would get him so wound up that he couldn't stand still.

In the winter of 1963 I had been transferred to Bow stables and on the occasion of Winston Churchill's funeral found myself among over 100 of the Mets 200 horses which were deployed along the ceremonial route from St Paul's Cathedral to the Thames at Tower Hill. This was where the great wartime leader was to be transferred from gun carriage to ceremonial barge to complete his final journey.

The route was lined with hundreds of people who stood in hushed respectful silence as the cortege approached. The only sound was the muffled drum beats of the escort when I became aware of the throbbing heart beat of Picador through the saddle flaps. This was not a good sign, his head was high and he couldn't have appeared more fearful as, in the hushed atmosphere, he took a deep breath and let fly with a whinny which could have been heard from St Paul's to the Tower of London. We sensibly withdrew to a nearby side street where he continued to call until the procession had passed.

In 1967 I was promoted to Sergeant and transferred to Hyde Park for a short period and while there came to the notice of Assistant Commissioner Sir John Waldron. Sir John was a great supporter of the Mounted Branch and unusually expressed a desire to get a police horse to qualify for the three day event at Badminton. This was something I dearly would have loved to have been involved in but it seemed to be reserved for the Remount Trainers at Imber Court.

While I was shepherding large and generally friendly crowds into Wembley Stadium or Arsenal football ground I would allow a moment, a fleeting wish, to be galloping across country before I would be jolted back into reality as we separated some group of the warring opponents or dealt with ticket touts, pick pockets, lost children and the like.

Although Sir John Waldron was one of the most high ranking police officers in the country it wasn't unusual to look up from grooming your horse to see him quietly standing in the aisle watching events in the stable.

My first meeting with him was when he appeared at Hyde Park Stables accompanied by our then head of Mounted Branch, Commander Alf Deats. They stopped outside the loose box as I was grooming Picador. Turning away from my horse and coming smartly to attention with body brush and curry comb in either hand I delivered the traditional police mantra of 'All correct Sir' as I desperately tried to keep my balance with Picador searching through my pockets.

I couldn't believe my luck as Sir John obviously recognized us from the Police Annual Horse Show and allowed me to sing Picador's praises. I boasted that he was super fit from his work in the forest and a natural jumper. 'What about his dressage?' asked Sir John. I could see the way the conversation was going and realized that this was my only chance of being considered for Eventing. Dressage was our weakest area but one I knew we could improve on. 'He's lovely to school and obedient' I replied, 'but needs some work on his flying changes.'

Sir John knew his horses and laughing at my cheek left the stable saying 'Get him in the team Mr. Deats'.

Some four hours later I received a dressing down by phone from the Chief Equitation Officer at Imber Court. Chief Inspector Albert Pilcher. Ex Royal Artillery, Albert had learnt his riding skills at the Army Riding School at Weedon. Both patient and knowledgeable, Albert was a man for whom I had a great deal of respect.

'Do you know what's involved in Eventing, the level of fitness required, what makes you think he can compete with some of the best Eventers in the country?' The questions came thick and fast as he expressed his doubts.

I wasn't going to let the chance slip away as I sang Picador's praises as being a bold jumper, fit, fast and as good as anything else the Mounted Branch had. Further more the Assistant Commissioner wanted a horse at Badminton and here was a strong contender.

Albert was clearly unimpressed but relented with, 'OK, bring him down on Monday and we'll have a look at him.'

Monday arrived and I happily set off on the twelve mile ride from Hyde Park to Imber Court where I was instantly taken under the wing of Assistant Equitation Instructor, Inspector Dennis Colton.

Dennis knew his dressage as well as anybody. Fellow of the British Horse Society and responsible for raising a best trained police horse class at the 'Horse of the Year show' he promptly put Picador and myself through our paces in the dressage ring before pronouncing that we were as good as the rest of the team.

'Badgy' had somewhat doubtfully registered us with the British Horse Society and entered us in the one day event at Stokenchurch in two weeks time bemoaning the fact that 'Picador would never win a one day event as long as he had a hole in his arse'. (Badgy never minced his words).

The next two weeks I trained with Bobby Hurford (also ex RHA and recent winner of a foxhunter class) and Geoff Dorset, Sergeant in charge of the remount section.

Came the day of the event and Picador went like a dream coming a respectable seventh in a field of 30. My competitors consisted of some experienced riders with a rich background in show jumping and Advanced Eventing.

There was no time to sit and dwell on any success as Picador and I were immediately back to normal duty performing crowd control at Wembley or patrolling the streets of the West End. But the die was cast and we found ourselves frequently called from duty to compete at various events on a weekend before back to duty on a Monday.

Badgy was delighted when Picador and I soon proved him wrong by winning a novice 'One Day Event' at Twesledown and imagine my delight when travelling to Hyde Park on the Central Line from Hainault while peeking over the shoulder of a fellow traveller to see in the sports pages of the Telegraph the headline. 'Picador, First for Police' followed by a most supportive article regarding our success.

After that we went on to qualify for the Three day Event at Badminton by being placed in the intermediate sections at

Twesledown and Whyly. I had my doubts about Badminton but was keen to take part. His dressage had improved tremendously though he had developed a 'String Halt' which marked him down a bit. His show jumping was never a problem and rarely collected any faults. His cross country was his strong point and he loved to gallop.

The 'Three day Event' with its steeplechase, roads and tracks and three and a half miles of cross country was a demanding test for the best horses in the country and for a police horse to take on such a challenge was unheard of. Badgy and Dennis Colton were quite rightly very nervous about taking such a step and after considerable debate we decided to enter him for Badminton but in the meantime try him in the advanced event at Twesledown which featured an advanced Dressage Test involving counter canters and extended trots. (but no flying changes,) a stiff show jumping course, and on the cross country day, a mile of steeplechase fences followed by several miles of roads and tracks and then over two miles of cross country, negotiating thirty fences of advanced height in the process. This was to be our defining moment, if he could complete the three day advanced event at Twesledown without injury then we would go for the International Three Day Event at Badminton.

I had an opportunity to school Picador round the practice fences of Twesledown including the steeplechase fences and water jumps. (Picador always hesitated before water taking away much of his momentum to sail over with abandon.) Three or four feet was never a problem but I could see the course builder had already built a ten foot stretch of water to jump in the forthcoming advanced event. To go near any of the prepared fences for a sneaky practice would have resulted in elimination before we even got to the event. Sadly I had no school master to give him a lead or tackle such an obstacle. He really needed a day's drag hunting but that was out of the question for a police horse.

Privately this caused me much concern, and then I remembered his old days alongside the river Roding in Chiwell where we regularly jumped a drainage ditch of some four feet. In those days as soon as we got into a canter alongside the stream with the drainage ditch coming into view he would spring into his stride before sailing over in fine style. If I could widen that ditch to seven or eight feet and approach it as normal he would be over before he knew it. However I doubted that the Council would have been too pleased about a Police Sergeant widening their ditches for the benefit of training a three day event horse.

There was nothing for it but to take a spade one dark night and do a bit of ditching on my own. By this time I had been transferred back to Chigwell as Sergeant. I figured that once the ditch was widened it was just a case of letting him approach it with his old confidence. The following day after my night time activities he did just that and he was over before he knew it, though he did have to stretch a bit. Thereafter he was much more fluent over wide stretches of water. In addition he had no problem jumping over obstacles into water.

With regular forest patrols, bags of road work toiling up the mile long rise of Palmerston Road in Buckhurst Hill and one day a week schooling around the cross country training course in Twesledown we were as ready as we could be for the Advanced event.

Picador was 'happy as Larry', super fit with no excess weight and extra rations, well down to his work and behaving far better in traffic, both he and I slept well at night. But the final chapter in our quest for Badminton was about to unravel.

Come the first day of the Twesledown advanced three day event there were over thirty top quality entrants featuring established riders such as Princess Anne, Mark Philips and my old Army Instructor and gold medalist Ben Jones. We performed an above average dressage test but I messed up the treble in the show jumping collecting eleven faults. The steeplechase, roads and tracks went without any problem but during the ten minute break before the cross country I was informed that many of the competitors were withdrawing.

Looking back I suspect that it was a deliberate ploy to save their best for Badminton but I also heard that some felt the track to be too firm and stony. Whatever the case my path was set. This was to be our test to see if we could cope with the most demanding of courses.

My main coach and mentor Badgy was unable to attend on the last day but had advised me beforehand just to school Picador round with no worries about time faults or finishing in a good position. So Dennis Colton was standing in, (cross country or any form of getting four legs off the ground was never Dennis's forte). I was only concerned in getting round, I wasn't bothered about time faults or finishing in the top ten so we took our time and approached each fence in a measured way giving Picador every chance. He went well until fence twenty seven a series of hedges and ditches involving a tight turn. Unusually for him he refused three times and was eliminated.

Jumping off and walking the last half mile in he started to show signs of lameness and clearly was feeling the going. He had given me everything he could and I couldn't have felt closer to him. We were even applauded as I led him back. I was greeted by a generous welcome from my friends and colleagues Bobby Hurford and Brian Dickinson who set to in making Picador as comfortable as possible with cold water bandages and wash down.

Sadly this was not the case with 'Chef d'Equipe' for the day Dennis Colton who I was to discover later was not our greatest fan. Standing over me as I removed Picador's studs he seemed more intent in getting my admission that Picador wasn't up to Badminton standards than concern for the horse.

As Badgy Pilcher and I had suspected we were not in the top class of Eventers but we has done our best to meet the Commissioner's wishes. We had been severely tested and found wanting but only just. Many of the top class Eventers had withdrawn from this event at the start of the cross country and more had retired or been eliminated on the way round. Indeed only seven horses of the thirty or so runners completed the course.

For a Police Horse earning his corn around the day to day duties of crowd control and daily police patrol he had been magnificent. Sir John Waldron sent a message of support together with a note to say Sergeant Petter and Picador are to be commended for their bravest efforts. To this day Picador still holds the record for being the only Police Horse ever to qualify and be entered for Badminton.

As I had qualified for Badminton I received an invitation to the pre event cocktail party where I would have been able to meet the other competitors but as we had withdrawn I just attended on the day of the cross country with my most supportive father and wife. It gave us a lift to see Picador's entry in the programme, he had received advanced favourable comments in the 'Horsey' magazines. It was within the crowds at each fence I overheard a comment "we will just see the police horse go through". It was with some sadness that I advised her of our withdrawal though she was delighted to get a first hand report on why we had withdrawn.

Picador soon recovered from his lameness and returned to ordinary duty where we happily continued working together for a couple of years before I was eventually allocated a new remount. As always was the case with the more mature horses he became the mount for a young recruit Mike Walker who always ruefully informed me that he could never pull him up in a tent pegging run and he was too spirited to be a good Police Horse.

There was always an argument that fit horses do not make the best Police Horses. It remains my view that a good Police Horse must be down to his work. He needs daily exercise, he needs to be fit and in good condition, to be well fed in a manner suitable to his work load, to receive daily grooming and attention from his regular rider and if all the foregoing is observed than you will get a good mount capable of easily dealing with the demands of daily duty.

In today's climate it has become fashionable to employ civilian grooms and there are some Police Forces around the world that use a system of making horses available for anyone to ride and take out on patrol as one would with signing out a police vehicle. Something that I can understand but it's my view that such a system never allows that rapport between horse and rider which is so important when the chips are down in a demanding and stressful situation such as a riot.

Since its reformation back in the 1920's under the guidance of Sir Percy Laurie the Metropolitan Police Mounted Branch had regularly patrolled the streets of London from as many as twenty six stables. Nevertheless all mounted officers and their mounts were regularly returned to the training establishment for Annual Training and during this time would engage in riding school and outdoor activities to improve obedience and iron out any vices.

In those days most of the recruits were ex military and had returned from Mounted Regiments in India or Palestine. Consequently they were adept at mounted tricks such as picking up a cap or handkerchief at the full gallop while leaning out the saddle. The early activity rides which featured at the Annual Horse Show and known as 'The Trick Ride' would demonstrate such skills along with Tent Pegging and Sword Lance and revolver events. As far as I could remember as far back as the 1960's there was a 36 horse musical ride under the control of a Mounted Inspector.

The Activity Ride which survives to this day was always under the control of the Chief Equitation Officer who I have seen produce horses that would curtsey to the crowd, jump through paper hoops and dive through fire as their riders removed their saddles. For several years Chief Inspector Alan Bingle produced a magnificent Activity Ride as well as a London Riding Clubs 'One Day Event' held in the back fields of Imber Court. Value for money? Better employed out on the streets? It's all questionable but the one thing such training always achieved was to produce a horse that was obedient, down to his work and a much improved control of their mounts as they dealt with day to day crowd control and police duty.

Copyright Nigel Norrington/Arena Pal

**The Metropolitan Police Show Jumping Team 1983
taken outside the officers mess St John's Wood Barracks.
PC's John Hayward on Dragoon, Nick White on Mountbatten
Len Parry on Gambit Mark Waller on Ingrid Together with
Police Commissioner Sir Kenneth and Lady Newman, Chief
Inspector Petter and Colonel Brian Kay T.A. H.A.C.**

Chapter Twelve

Public Order and Crowd Control.

Apart from their 'day to day' tasked patrols on the streets of London, it's fair to say a great proportion of a Mounted Officer's work is policing large crowds in public order situations, particularly at football stadiums and the like.

During the 70's and 80's a hooligan element developed where it seemed to us that each game was an opportunity to avenge old grievances against visiting teams or just good sport to lay in wait for the opposition to emerge while the home team lay in ambush.

It wasn't unusual for London's Mounted Branch being required to provide aid to three major football stadiums plus an event at Wembley and a public order demonstration all on the same day. This meant that the overall requirement would exceed over 100 horses. The normal mounted contingent would comprise one Inspector, one Sergeant and ten Police Constables but on the more busy games it wasn't unusual to field a team of One Inspector Two Sergeants and Twenty Constables.

Normally the presence of uniformed officers escorting groups of visitors from the local underground station or coach park to and from the ground would be sufficient to maintain law and order. But the general public would be amazed if they were to witness some of the hooliganism that did erupt once a local gang ambushed a rival team of supporters.

The mindless antics of these young gangs would result in a high street being witness to running fights and terror of shoppers with children taking refuge wherever they could. Gangs would pursue other groups simply for displaying the wrong colours. Some gangs would take cover in shops only to be chased through the premises while the staff did their best to protect shoppers and goods for sale which were being grabbed in the melee.

On one occasion after a game, (which the home side probably lost) we were escorting Manchester United visitors from Tottenham Football Stadium to Seven Sisters Underground Station, a walk of about a mile. The visitors just wanted to get safely home while the worst of the home side supporters made lunges at them from either side as they jeered and threw debris. The mindless mob were committing no end of criminal offences. The few accompanying foot duty officers soon disappeared as they made their arrests leaving the Mounted Branch to complete the journey.

I found myself a walking centre of refuge as the fans clustered around my horse for protection and whenever I found it necessary to drive off the gangs of would be attackers the terrified victims would beg me to stay with them.

Mounted Branch were getting well spread out as each of us dealt with their own immediate situations. In my case there was nothing for it but to treat the station yard at Tottenham as a place of refuge. Leaving the terrified group there, I advised them to wait until the gangs were dispersed while I continued with the escort to Seven Sisters. As was often the case in these situations one could identify a main ringleader but it was always prudent to choose your moment to make an arrest. In my case, once we arrived at Seven Sisters Underground Station I was able to instruct the foot duty to arrest one such moron who had been a ringleader from the start.

Returning to Tottenham Police Station to charge my prisoner, I was amazed to find the yard still full of Manchester United Supporters. They took some convincing that the streets were now clear and it was safe for them to continue their journey.

I must admit that the uneasy feeling of not being able to give them complete faith for their continued safety left me feeling inadequate and frustrated. However the sight that met my eyes as I entered the charge room filled me with pride as I found several other Mounted Officers charging their prisoners. The local Deputy

Assistant Commissioner was so impressed with our work that we received a letter of commendation the following week.

Such behaviour is not so likely in today's climate. Intelligence gathering is much more sophisticated and with the massive surveillance provided by CCTV even the mob have come to realize that they will be identified and subsequently charged after the event.

Over the years I served and to this day, Mounted Branch demonstrate their ability to police on horse back. Public order played a large part in our daily routine but the majority of our time was spent on daily patrols during which we could encounter any type of police duty that our foot duty colleagues experienced. Of course our inability to enter buildings restricted our response but over the years Mounted Police have successfully arrested criminals for an endless variety of offences ranging from assault, house breaking, theft from cars and even attempted murder.

When I joined Mounted Branch in 1963 there were no traffic wardens and few traffic lights. Police were expected to report any traffic offences from parking through to uninsured or unlicenced driving offences. Consequently a Constable's work rate was judged not only on his ability on horseback and interaction with the public but also included his ability to issue a summons. (Note. The word 'his', we had no female officers in the Mounted Branch until 1971.) A weekly return would be gathered on each area and a central record of work performed by Mounted Branch would be forwarded to the Commissioner's Office.

There were several officers laughingly referred to as 'Uniform Carriers' and although we were always trained on new legislation and changes in police practice, some officers hadn't attended court for years as they became more and more detached from practical police duty. The subsequent unpopular policy of interchange between departments at regular periods throughout a constable's career to some extent, restored and broadened their all round ability.

There were several landmark events where Mounted Branch played a major part in policing public disturbances. Normally, demonstrations would have a political theme and for the most part we spent many hours 'standing by' in some side-street before being dismissed without deployment.

Events where we were used to good effect included:-

Grosvenor Square antiwar in Vietnam protest on the 17th March 1968. Perhaps this was the beginning of a new policy emerging regarding riot gear and personal protection, for on this occasion, a breakaway group of several hundred demonstrators tried to attack the American Embassy. Police officers in normal uniform, suddenly found themselves under missile, or should I say debris attack?

Various Campaign for Nuclear Disarmament protests during the 70's.

Lewisham Riots 1977 where Anti Nazi league clashed with National Front.

Anti vivisection demos, Carshalton.

Red Lion Square 15th June 1974, where the International Marxist Group, The International Socialist Group and other groups clashed with the National Front.

Southall 23rd April 1979. Where the Anti Nazi League demonstrated against the National Front outside the Town Hall (Over one hundred horses on reserve.)

Grundwick's dispute 1976 -1978 Where Chief Inspector John West, the only person with a radio was tipped off his horse leaving me as Inspector in charge with no communication before a harassed Chief Superintendent was able to climb on some railings to mouth the words 'go away' or something like that. I remember it was definitely two words.

Wapping Printers' dispute, nightly for over a year1986-87.

Poll Tax Riots 1st April 1990. Where mounted officers had to be reinforced by further serials deployed on major football deployments.

There seemed to be an unending requirement for the use of Mounted Branch and as an Operational Chief Inspector I was constantly juggling with figures to produce officers and sound horses to a number of events on the same day. We would normally ride to such locations but often, hired horse transport had to be used as we only had two horse boxes.

Add to the foregoing requirements the constant demand for mounted aid on ceremonial events such as 'Trooping the Colour,' 'State Visits,' 'The opening of Parliament,' Royal Weddings, a Papal visit and the like. Our lives were varied and fulfilling.

As late as the early 1990's we were still working out of more than twenty stables located around London. This placement or location of stables was a natural evolvement brought about from the times when each police station had its own horse transport before the arrival of the motor car.

The comradeship was terrific, like all major corporations The Mounted Branch had a great social club, its own sports teams, even a choir. And every Christmas the staff would produce a brilliant pantomime performed in The City of London Police Station for the benefit of our own and handicapped children.

We even had a Pentathlon Team, formed by Station Police Sergeant John Moore and gladly supported by myself if only for the competitive riding event. We competed at National Level and found ourselves up against the Olympic teams of the day.

The annual Metropolitan Police horse show held over two days at Imber Court was almost the Commissioner's garden party. A grand affair with competing teams from all mounted branches from across the country, The Metropolitan Police Band and displays by the Dog Section plus a musical ride and activity ride all added to the occasion. The organisation of this annual event required extra stabling at Sandown Park and Hampton Court and probably took

74

more than two hundred officers off the streets for more than a week.

But times were changing. Departmental scrutiny, a 'nothing sacred' ethos concentrating on value for money and civilianization wherever possible saw the small stables disappear as more efficient larger stables took their place. Riot gear has become commonplace. Today in 2016, reductions in manpower have seen the Branch cut from 201 horses to 120. Foot duty cordons with riot shields are more prominent and more emphasis is concentrated on alternative means of dispersing rioting crowds.

I must admit a constant enthusiasm for all of it. I loved practical police duty and although a qualified British Horse Society Instructor never felt the urge to leave the streets and join the staff at Imber Court until I became head of the Branch in 1993.

Chapter Thirteen
Ceremonial and Royalty.

A major responsibility of the police in central London was the overall supervision and policing of public order and ceremonial events. Consequently the force required a large contingent of Mounted Branch who would be required on a daily basis to escort movement of Troops as they 'Changed the Guard' or on such occasions as a State Visit. Normally the stables at Great Scotland Yard, Rochester Row and Hyde Park with their combined establishment of forty horses between them could cater for ninety per cent of the demands. Daily Guard Changes, escort of the Household Cavalry, presentation of letters of credence by Ambassadors to Buckingham Palace and minor public order event were all covered by the Mounted Branch Officers who jokingly referred to themselves as 'The Royal A'.

Where the demands of the day required more mounted support such as 'Trooping the Colour' mounted officers would ride in from stables further afield.

In the summer, daily guard changes were a major tourist attraction and it was not unusual to identify pickpockets or unacceptable touching by petty criminals. Mounted officers were able to see separated distressed children and reunite them with parents.

All this was going on as Troops were escorted down from Chelsea Barracks or brought over from nearby Wellington Barracks. On State occasions the King's Troop Royal Horse Artillery were escorted down from St John's Wood to fire Royal

Salutes in Hyde Park. The Mounted Bands of the Household Cavalry all added to the scene and the Mounted Branch was very much part of it.

Chief Inspector Petter riding Police Horse 'Kathleen'
State visit 1989

On State Visits and 'Opening of Parliament' the Mounted Branch were required to provide a four horse grey escort with an Inspector leading the procession and a four horse escort bringing up the rear. There was great pride in being selected for the Grey Escort and much care was given to ensure the grey horses and their respective riders matched for colour and height. The Inspector would be in constant radio contact with the control centre and would divert the route in the event of an emergency. The pace was to be set by the Monarch's carriage which in turn predicted the pace of the accompanying Household Cavalry which in turn was judged by the Police Inspector leading the Grey Escort. I would set off from Victoria Station or Buckingham Palace with everyone falling into their respective slots in the procession at a sitting trot (to post in the saddle was frowned upon) and somehow keep an eye on the following procession as we spread out along Victoria Street and Whitehall. At times the lead riders of the Cavalry would close up and at others lag behind dependent on circumstances down the line.

Covert Mounted Branch support was provided to the Royal Mews and it was quite a surprise to see the odd colleague dressed in the full livery of the Royal Household strutting around the Royal Mews.

Because of their constant contact with ceremonial events and crowd control the Mounted Branch were blessed in so much as they had many suitable mounts who could be relied upon to behave in a sedate manner when all this pomp and ceremony was going on. For many years the Queen would ride side saddle down the Mall and on to Horse Guards Parade on her mounts 'Imperial' and 'Burmese.' They were regularly used for police duty as they were made ready for the forthcoming ceremonial events. Sir John Miller, The Crown Equerry, would provide what horses he could from the Royal Mews for the various high ranking officers who would ride on the parade as Colonels of Regiments and the like. But each year there would be a request to the Metropolitan Police to provide additional suitable mounts.

At Superintendent level I was required to attend the Royal Mews with a selection of suitable mounts while the Colonel would mentally match horses with royal and senior military. Then for the next six weeks or so it wouldn't be unusual to see such pairings out riding while they got to know their allocated mounts.

Come the big day of the Trooping the gates leading into the palace gardens would be opened and I would walk with the whole assembly of saddled horses and carriages through the back gardens and round to the inner quadrangle of the palace where various high ranking officials would be united with their various mounts. Once mounted and in position a hush would descend on the gathering as The Queen would emerge to ride side saddle or in later years take her carriage down the Mall. In the meantime together with mounted police grooms and the rest of the Royal Mews staff I would jump into a waiting palace minibus while we set off in a mad dash down Birdcage Walk to arrive on Horse Guards Parade in time to take up my allocated slot at the back of the parade. In the event of one of our police horses playing up I could call out one of the grooms to assist with remounting or removal Etc., In the five years I performed this duty not once did we have to remove a horse or remount a fallen officer, surely a tribute to skill and dedication of the mounted officers who prepared the horses.

Once Her Majesty rode off the parade ground there would be another mad dash down birdcage walk and into the inner courtyard where a much more relaxed atmosphere would prevail. Once dismounted it was quite normal for the children of the various nobility to jump up and be led round the yard prior to taking their place on the balcony for the Fly-past.

There was no doubt that ceremonial duties had to be precise and perfectly presented, a removal from everyday policing but very much a part of the London Scene. It always seemed to me that Mounted Branch Officers were proud to be so heavily involved with it.

Chapter Fourteen

Women Police Officers On Horseback-
Surely Not!

By the time of the Westminster Bridge incident Women Police on horseback was commonplace, they regularly turned out for public order events with their male colleagues and it was considered quite normal. After all it's the horse that is the effective piece of equipment and provided the rider is competent, a mounted officer should be able to perform all their duties regardless of their sex.

Such thinking wasn't always the case, when I joined in 1959 male officers represented 90 percent of the force with just two female officers to each station. My initial training class in 1959 of twenty constables consisted of 17 male officers and just 3 women police officers. Their duties at station consisted of mainly dealing with women and children and were never used on normal patrol duties or seen driving the few vehicles that we had. To be part of any specialized section apart from the rare exception within the CID was unheard of. Consequently there were no female officers in Traffic Patrol, Mounted Branch, Dog Section or any other specialist squads.

But as the song goes 'The times they were a changing' in today's climate it seems odd that there ever could have been such segregation. Today, women in all walks of life are almost equal in numbers to the men and in the Mounted Police now outnumber the male officers. I was astonished (and proud) when my own daughter measuring just five feet two inches asked me to go running with her to get fit for her assessment to join the Met. She is still serving some 20 years later and somehow raising a family of three children.

In 1971 the Mounted Branch made history with the recruitment of its first Women Police Constables Ann McPhereson and Margaret Goodacre. Today, in 2017, the branch is led by its first female Chief Inspector, Helen O'Sullivan.

The King's Troop Royal Horse Artillery has seen its first female Commanding officer. Today in 2016, I am informed that the Household Cavalry now has more female Troopers than male.

The most demanding Three Day Event is full of professional horse women, Princess Anne has won an Olympic gold medal. Dressage, Cross Country, Horse Racing, even the Grand National all have female riders.

The early ominous forewarnings of 'They will just be uniform carriers, never make an arrest or complete a summons report on horseback, or can't be used in public disorder' have all been shown to be a nonsense as they go about the same duties as their male colleagues.

Towards the end of my service in 1994 I was regularly interviewing applicants for the branch. We would normally be looking for 6 recruits every six months to maintain the Branch strength. The quality of the female applicants was outstanding both in educational achievements and riding skills as they had all in the main been avid Pony Club members in their youth.

On the other hand the male recruit rarely had previous riding experience. However they were always very fit with a good record of achievement, quick to learn and by the end of the training course were every bit as competent as those officers with previous experience.

Selection always had to be on merit and we reached a point where the Branch attracted two thirds female applicants to one third male. Such was the success of the female applicants that I could foresee a time where positive discrimination would need to be introduced to avoid the Branch becoming a female only department.

Chapter Fifteen
A Ghostly Place

Hounslow Heath could be a bleak and windswept place in the heart of winter. Walkers would have been astonished at the town that suddenly appeared upon its marshes back in the 1980's in the space of a few weeks. However this was no ordinary town, surrounded by high fences and coils of barbed wire the walker would notice that there were no people, the only sign of traffic was a burnt out motor car or two, the shops and houses were all immaculate with highly painted facades but to try and enter most of them would bring about the realization that this town was virtually a Hollywood film set.

Deserted and ghostly, a walker could walk the perimeter fence on a misty morning and be forgiven if he felt that some strange plague had wiped out humanity. On another day however he would have been astonished as a line of shield carrying riot police came running round the corner followed by a line of Police Horses at a rapid trot or even a controlled canter. He would have been further dismayed to see a mob of people emerge from a side street to hurl wooden blocks and tennis balls in an attack on the riot control force before he realized that he was witnessing a training exercise in crowd control for police horses.

The ghost town is no longer there, a new housing estate stands in its place, such training has since been removed to a new site in Kent. The purpose of the site was to equip officers in use of shields in crowd control or protection against other forms of attack. All Mounted Officers would regularly train with foot duty serials as they rehearsed crowd dispersal techniques in accordance with Home Office guidelines.

Much of a mounted police officers role in crowd control is to direct the crowds in busy situations such as a football match at Wembley or many of the major football grounds around the country. In a densely packed crowd it is far easier for an officer on horseback to direct a crowd than it is for their foot duty colleagues who cannot be seen so well. In such situations Mounted Police can work with the goodwill of the crowd who appreciate the assistance given in ensuring their safety and preventing injury. The horse is trained to work in a passive way standing for hours where necessary or forming queues or gently moving crowds by use of the 'half pass' where the horse moves sideways into the crowd.

During the miners' strike of 1984 a large demonstration organized by the TUC was marching on Downing Street and had completely filled up Whitehall with demonstrators some of whom were being arrested for public order offences. As Inspector in charge and waiting on reserve in the stables at New Scotland Yard with a mounted complement of two Sergeants and twenty constables a total of twenty three horses including my own, I kept a keen ear to my personal radio for any calls for assistance.

Such waiting on reserve was normal procedure on all the major demonstrations and normally resulted in Mounted Branch being dismissed without being deployed. However over the years one developed a sixth sense on whether things were going to deteriorate and in such cases I would take the precaution of giving the order to 'Girth up' and be ready to mount up at short notice. This order would result in feedbags being removed if still on, bridles being replaced. Mounted Officers would leave their refreshments untouched as they checked saddles and prepared for a possible deployment.

On this occasion I was listening to developments on my personal radio when the phone rang. It was Central Control, "Gold Commander instructs that you are to enter Whitehall via Whitehall Place and disperse the crowds at your discretion". An unusual instruction but one, which showed the trust the Commander had in our conduct and discipline.

As usual the great majority of the demonstrators were peaceful. Although noisy and boisterous they were legitimately carrying out their right to demonstrate, hold meetings and present petitions. As we approached Whitehall I could see women and children on the demonstration and called the detail to a halt while I dismounted and walked out into Whitehall to assess the situation.

This to me was an occasion where we could use the goodwill of the public and direct them to the best way to avoid trouble and get transport home. Returning to the Mounted Serial I informed the officers what to expect and how we would use our mounts in the same way as we would in a large crowd at a peaceful football match.

The officers knew exactly what was required of them and it was with considerable pride that I witnessed the good will and atmosphere that developed as they directed the people to the Embankment and home.

Rarely would horses be used in a more forceful manner for crowd dispersal although over the years there have been occasions when Mounted Police have been used to break up aggressive mobs bent on public disorder or criminal damage. It's in these situations that correctly trained personnel and horses are so useful in maintaining order and preventing riots.

In 1963 during the Vietnam War the American Embassy in Grosvenor Square came under attack by demonstrators trying to force their way in. There were no riot shields or protective equipment for man or horse in those days. The police officers helmet was the only protection against missiles. Mounted officers didn't even wear hard hats. A soft peaked cap was deemed to be sufficient. I was taking the Sergeant's exam that day and missed the demo but the following day I was enthralled by accounts from foot duty officers of how the Mounted Branch had 'saved the day'.

The public order training at Hounslow was designed to rehearse various moves employed by Mounted Branch in controlling or dispersing crowds under both passive and violent conditions. In the case of the latter Home Office regulations state that 'In the event of major disorder it may be necessary for mounted police to conduct a dispersal by approaching a crowd in a controlled manner at the walk, trot or even faster paces giving the impression that they do not intend to stop. In such cases they will only advance to a predetermined line set by the senior mounted officer in command'. Over the years all Mounted Officers received this instruction and training until the movement became ingrained into our minds as second nature. Foot duty officers with shields would train with mounted officers and rehearse the moment when they would split and separate to allow horses to surge through and break up a riot.

Timing was critical and procedure demanded that we should inform the crowd of our intention to use horses to disperse them. This would be done by use of loud hailer from hand held megaphones or over the loud speakers mounted on vehicles if possible.

It was on one such occasion that as Senior Officer in charge of Mounted Branch that I was instructed to form a cordon across Westminster Bridge to prevent students taking the wrong route on their agreed protest march.

The stewards directing the demonstrators had been unable to keep the marchers to the agreed prescribed route of keeping to the south bank of the Thames until reaching Lambeth Bridge. It seemed that the sight of the Houses of Parliament across Westminster Bridge was too attractive to them and so led to a disregard of their own stewards and to an illegal rush over the bridge. A cordon of foot duty and police vehicles was hastily put in place to prevent a surge on Parliament while I was directed by Silver Command Dave Richards to form a Mounted cordon behind the police vehicles.

It was very nearly a lost situation before we were able to bring the surge to a halt about half way across the bridge. For the next two hours we sat on our horses as we tried various forms of instruction and persuasion to move the crowd back to the South Bank. The students were mainly good natured and even moved back a little so the police vehicles were withdrawn. I remember having a good-natured discussion with several students during the afternoon, as indeed did the rest of the mounted serial. (The horses were always popular with the public). Nevertheless as the afternoon wore on the students became more and more restless as they tested the strength of the cordon by forming unruly groups to break through in the weaker areas.

Westminster Bridge is a wide road with room for two lanes of traffic flowing either way plus generous pavements on either side but a line of twenty or so of horses makes a solid, albeit restless barrier across the street. Various moves were made to persuade the crowd to revert to the approved route but they were having none of it. We tried withdrawing the mounted cordon and replacing with foot cordons and police vehicles; announcements were constantly being made to the crowd to retrace their steps to the South Bank.

Matters were rapidly going downhill, arrests were being made and the crowd was becoming more and more violent as time wore on. Mounted Branch had tried to persuade the crowd to retreat by advancing at the walk into the crowd but was ineffective as the crowd became more aggressive. Police vehicles were drawn up behind the Mounted Branch as we were instructed to fall back behind the vehicles and it became obvious that we would have to disperse in a more robust manner.

It was at this point that Deputy Assistant Commissioner Tony Speed took control and instructed the vehicles to move to the kerbs, it was obvious to us all that Mounted Branch were about to be called in. I quickly shouted to the serial that it looked like we were about to be deployed and that we would approach in line at the trot, no one was to go past the stone lion statues at the South end of the bridge. I had to smile when I heard several voices call out 'Whatdesay, Whatdesay?' and, 'Sir! Sir!, the Guvner's calling us in.' I again repeated the instructions as Tony Speed was making hand signals from 50yards away for us to advance.

It was now that our many hours of training kicked in and I had every confidence that the mounted officers and the control of their horses would be superb. We advanced line abreast at a strong but steady trot and it was heartening to see the students at last getting the message as they surged back over the bridge and dispersed. Apart from one injury to the public where a hefty lady was trodden on when one horse came down on the metalled road surface, the dispersal worked beautifully and was a tribute to our horse, our training and the horsemanship of the officers.

As was always the case in such situations there was to be a debrief at Scotland Yard and after turning my horse in it was heartening to receive a round of applause from the serial commanders as I made my late entry into the briefing room. I took this to be an acknowledgement for all the mounted officers on duty that afternoon. A message that was a pleasure to pass on to all concerned over the following few days.

Predictably an inquiry was hurriedly set up by an outside force to investigate the whole days events and particularly the events leading up to and during the dispersal.

So within a couple of days I found myself with DAC Tony Speed before the inquiry team quoting line and verse from the home office manual regarding the use of police horses in crowd dispersal.

The inquiry completely endorsed our action and we came away with the feeling that given the circumstances the situation couldn't have been handled better. The sound training and practised routines at Hounslow Heath had paid off and ensured that our training and discipline had been a major factor in maintaining the peace.

Chapter Sixteen

'Police Horses Are Bombproof...Aren't They?'

Empress hated red buses

One of the main criticisms emerging from the use of police horses at the Wapping Printers' dispute was the use of unauthorized equipment, namely riding crops. Mounted officers are equipped with a small short truncheon, which is carried in the wallets on the saddle and a three-foot long cane baton, which is slung on the side of the saddle.

The use of the long baton is approved under Home Office regulations and only to be resorted to under extreme circumstances. This measure was not resorted to on the night of the 24th January. To ride with one hand on the reins while the other holds an unwieldy long stick leads to a certain sacrifice of control of the horse. The horse responds to hand and leg and the use of both hands will keep the animal under tighter control. The order to draw long truncheons is a practised drill and as officer in charge that night I would have had to give that order. Although the mob was extremely violent and had to be dispersed I felt that the use of truncheons would have reduced our efficiency, a fact that I discussed with Sergeant Rouse who cheerfully agreed that he wanted both hands on the reins.

I have always admired the skill and courage demonstrated by riders at Cheltenham or going over Beechers Brook in the Grand National. Similarly the fearless way jockeys ride across country in Eventing or 'Point to Point'. Show Jumping and Polo all demand a great measure of empathy with one's mount.

Many people believe that all Police Horses are 'Bombproof' namely that you can lead them into the most hostile or frightening environment and they will remain unperturbed and quietly stand or stroll for hours on end with no reaction other than a flicked ear or idle gaze.

Nothing could be further from the truth. London abounds in hazards and nuisances that at times seem designed to turn the most seasoned police horse into a frenzied runaway. It's only their training and solid temperament that ensures their safety and that of the rider and public. One minute one could be riding down a quiet side street when a sudden whoosh of falling debris will crash into a roadside skip as construction workers empty a wheelbarrow into a chute three floors above your head. Heavy vehicles, claxons and sirens all add to the noise of London's traffic. Military bands fireworks and crowds all add to the scary scene that awaits the young horse when he first leaves the Mounted Training

Establishment at Imber Court. It's a tribute to the Mounted Police officer that he can patrol 365 days a year with such an impressive safety record.

On a windy day I've experienced galvanized corrugated sheets of metal being torn off the sides of construction sites and following me down the road as if they have a will of their own and is determined to get me.

In the early days of leaving the training school a young horse would normally be accompanied by a solid stable mate who would instill confidence while the 'Remount' as it's known would get their first sight of their new environment. In a short time however the young horse should settle and become a safe ride on its own.

Nevertheless each horse has its own idiosyncrasies and its regular rider would learn what to watch out for and find their own way of overcoming or avoiding such problems.

Some horses would 'Napp' and turn away from an approaching dustcart or fire engine with claxon sounding. Such behaviour was understandable to the experienced rider who would normally have been selected for his skill in understanding the young horse's mind.

Sometimes a soothing word would be sufficient to quell the fear in Dobbin's mind, other times a more urgent 'Go on' might be needed. A horse spinning away from an approaching heavy goods vehicle could be a danger to all concerned.

Over time the horse's regular rider would find various tactics that would work for their individual mounts. To keep a horse going forward rather than fleeing could be the difference between safety and chaos.

A common solution to such a nightmare was to carry a small stick or light crop which although not standard issue could be approved under certain circumstances. Such was the situation for a small number of riders at Wapping.

All mounted officers can recall amusing or even dangerous situations whereby their appointed horse could be almost guaranteed to dig his heels in and refuse point blank to go forward or side step in an elegant half pass at the trot or even faster as they surge past an imagined danger. Some would spin or even rear and it never failed to impress me how many colleagues would, upon hearing of such antics would say with tongue in cheek "Never does it with me" or "You must be pushing the wrong buttons" etc.

One such horse issued to me was 'Empress' a lovely chestnut with some Suffolk Punch in her. Gentle by nature, willing and good in crowds her only vice was that she hated red buses, which in London one would think was a major disadvantage. However by using common sense and a watchful eye on the road ahead one could keep out of trouble. She would pass a stationary bus, exercising a dainty half pass, but if the driver pulled away just as you were passing your dainty half pass could require two or three lanes of traffic much to the consternation of London's drivers.

On one such occasion I was returning to Hyde Park stables from a visit to the Forge at Hammersmith, when I was overtaken by a large lorry towing an equally large flatbed trailer, a combined length of about 40 yards. The lorry then stopped with its trailer poking into the two- lane carriageway. Empress strolled calmly by without turning a hair. I stopped by the cab and advised the driver to straighten up a bit as his tail end was causing obstruction. Whilst engaged in conversation I noticed that the lorry seemed to be moving forward; far from it, unnoticed by me and while I was speaking, the passing traffic had come to a halt leaving a dreaded red bus immediately alongside Empress's head on my right, unable to perform her elegant half pass through lack of space and refusing to move forward her only route was backwards which she somehow managed to achieve at impossible speed. My problems were only just beginning, the space into which she was reversing was reducing in width and behind the bus was a waiting car, no spurring on or shouting could convince Empress that the safest route was to go forward and to the astonishment and horror of the car driver her hocks hit the car front bumper and radiator. Surely the only way for me to go was straight through the windscreen and onto the lap of the now deathly white-faced driver.

Don't ask me how, someone had once told me that horses always seem to find an extra leg some how and this occasion illustrated the point brilliantly. Having hit the radiator of the car and being squeezed between the bus and the trailer, Empress's only way was up. Sitting on the bonnet of the car like some circus elephant pawing the air with her front legs and with me clinging to her neck she was able to swing her legs over the flat bed and clamber over the car and onto the pavement. There seemed to be much clanging and banging as Empress's new shoes climbed over the car but amazingly she never fell and somehow I had stayed in the saddle. By this time the bus and lorry had pulled away leaving the poor car driver close to cardiac arrest.

Concerned for both car driver and horse I jumped off to inspect the damage. Surely she was injured; surely the car bonnet was flattened. But no, incredibly Empress had sustained a slight cut to her hocks and the car bonnet had just one horseshoe imprint with a neat Mordax stud mark and scratch.

The visibly shaken driver was kindness itself. In spite of his scare he showed the utmost concern for the horse apologized for driving so close to the lorry and refused to make any fuss over his damage.

A completely unconcerned Empress strolled into Hyde Park stables looking for her next meal while I was regaled with "You must be pushing the wrong buttons" and "Never happens to me".

Chapter Seventeen

Dragoon Teaches Me A Lesson

During my service with London's Mounted Branch we were often fortunate in that we were joined by officers who had previous riding experience in the Army. Such personnel were extremely experienced in all matters equine, were extremely proficient horsemen, and well disciplined.

During the 1970's I was posted as Mounted Inspector to West Hampstead, a lovely ground for Mounted Police work. Within riding distance of Wembley Stadium, Tottenham and Arsenal football grounds with their frequent demands for Mounted Branch for crowd control. The stables were just a stone's throw from Hampstead Heath where a patrolling officer could keep the heath safe from crime while at the same time exercise his horse on the riding tracks.

It was here that I was first to meet 'Dragoon' and his appointed rider 'John', a man with previous mounted experience in the Household Cavalry. An imposing figure! Six foot two inches tall, who still managed to keep his weight under the unwritten maximum weight requirement of thirteen and a half stone.

A most competent horseman who kept us all amused with his zany humour and 'Benny Hill' salutes. Outgoing and popular with the public he could always be relied upon to turn a boring afternoon standing on reserve into some sort of entertainment. On one such occasion whilst standing on reserve during the 'Brixton Race Riots' as they became known, I was returning from a briefing in the operations room and was astonished to see John smiling broadly walking into the back yard with a massive television that had been dropped by a gang who had raided a shop and fled straight into the arms of a line of ten Mounted Officers. "Proceeds of crime Sir" he explained cheerfully. "And you're going to book it in as 'property found in the street', correct?" "Of course" was his implacable reply as he headed for the stables.

As I have mentioned earlier, not all horses were bombproof, whether it was through lack of courage, inexperience or in some cases sheer high spirits. In Dragoon's case as a young remount, it was the latter. Dragoon could unseat his rider if given the chance by dropping his head and almost clapping his hind heels above the rider's head as he went into a series of bucks, leaps and swerves which would have been a hit in any rodeo ring.

Consequently, when he first came out to duty under John's expert tuition, only John rode him for his early introduction to London's traffic. It was normal in such cases for a remount to be accompanied by a quiet and mature schoolmaster who hopefully would induce a feeling of calm and discipline into the behaviour of the young horse.

Having been out to duty for a couple of weeks and unaware of his 'Rodeo routine' I volunteered to give John a day off by taking Dragoon up to Hampstead Heath whereupon he promptly went into a series of loud screams and whinnies as he tried to locate a kindred spirit.

Anxious to settle him down I schooled him for twenty minutes or so on a flat area of grass before deciding to let him stretch a bit on the sandy ride surrounding the heath. It was at this moment I discovered his 'Rodeo Routine' as he sprang into a strong canter shouting his head off before going into a series of bucks, props and swerves before pitching me between his ears and promptly stopping to graze at the side of the track.

Remounting I could hear the words of Ben Jones my old riding instructor at the King's Troop, "Grab the front arch of the saddle, keep his head up and kick him on". For the next five minutes Dragoon thrilled the walkers on the Heath with his contortions and antics while I grimly pulled myself into the saddle and pushed him on before he settled into a smooth canter and returned calmly to the stable.

I was somewhat miffed when upon explaining my experience the next day at John's mock expressions of surprise and incredulity and his laughing "It never happens to me, you must be pushing the wrong buttons", was predictable. His comments were to come back to haunt him when some week or two later at a training session on the Heath, Dragoon managed to dispatch him three times in a row with me using the benefit of my recent experience shouting 'Grab the front arch of the saddle and kick him on.' It was obvious that John had no faith in my solution as he bravely remounted and attempted to master this bucking bronco. It was painful to watch and even more painful for John as each time he hit the ground I became more and more concerned for his safety.

Not half of the concern I felt when upon rising from his third fall he uttered those words every riding instructor experiences when giving a lesson, "Guvner, can you show me?"

In actual fact I was glad that he did because my earlier experience with Dragoon gave me every confidence that I had the answer to this maverick and although not in riding gear was delighted to jump up and demonstrate how to sit out his contortions. The gathered observers and rest of the riders went quiet as I accepted John's request, you could almost feel their anticipation as they looked forward to another crashing fall. They were unaware that I had already worked out the answer to Dragoon's shenanigans. I had no doubt that I could sit out his antics although aware that things could go wrong. Sure enough as I changed from trot to canter on a circle Dragoon performed a leap into the air with arched back and attempting to buck on landing, his attempt to drop his head failed as I lifted the reigns, grabbed the front arch and vigorously kicked him on. Another few strides in canter before another buck this time followed by an attempt to swerve. I kept him cantering on the circle before changing the reign. Sure enough he tried it again but Ben Jones' advice stood me in good stead as Dragoon sated his enthusiasm and obediently fell into a controlled canter. Visibly impressed and much recovered John again jumped up and it was a delight to see him master Dragoons high spirits by using this simple technique of grabbing the pommel.

With his new found confidence John and Dragoon became quite an attraction as they demonstrated their rodeo act at the Metropolitan Police Horse Show and they went on to perform with great credit at the Royal Tournament and various shows and events.

Dragoon eventually settled down and was selected for the prestigious 'Grey Escort' on ceremonial parades and performed well in crowds at public order.

Chapter Eighteen

Joe Destroys Crime Scene And Rotten Row In The 70's

Rotten Row during the 70's was a constant scene of equine activity. Horse Guards Drilling, local riding schools and private riders schooling and exercising, carriages from the Royal Mews all working along it's three miles or more of sandy all weather tracks. Bordered by the Serpentine and the park itself, it was quintessentially English to the core.

Placed in the centre of London and surrounded by the roads of Park Lane, Kensington, South Carriage Road and Bayswater Road it was overlooked by expensive hotels, Embassies and the most up-market residences.

At the time the Metropolitan Police had a police station in the very heart of this wonderful setting. Together with its 10 horse stable, Hyde Park Police Station was a prime posting for any Mounted Officer.

It was during the 70's that an embassy official was murdered while sitting in his car outside the Iranian Embassy and directly adjacent to the South ride in Kensington Gore. A crime investigation scene was quickly set up with the immediate area cordoned off from the public with blue and white police tape. Part of the restricted area spread onto the horse ride where C.I.D. officers conducted a fingertip search on their hands and knees as they searched for empty cartridge cases or anything that might be connected with the crime.

It was at the same time that police horse Joe stepped out of his Hyde Park stable together with his new rider John. John had only recently arrived to his new posting and as such was getting to know the various horses in the stable. Young and enthusiastic, new to the Mounted Branch John was on a high learning curve. He was slightly different from your average police entrant. Public school educated from a very Country Farming Set from the borders of South West Surrey and West Sussex. John very quickly became popular and good company. He soon became Captain of the Branch Cricket team, took part in Mounted Drill and threw himself into every aspect of Mounted Branch Duty.

Police horse 'Joe' however was a seasoned police horse, snow white with flowing mane and considerable Arab in his breeding. A bit on the small side for a police horse who, given his head could go like the wind and looked like something out of 'Lawrence of Arabia'. Nevertheless on patrol or escort duty Joe was a delight to ride and behaved perfectly. "Just don't let him get into a spin on the rides" came the helpful advice from his Sergeant Wally Davies as Joe commenced his patrol.

Crossing the Dell Bridge by the Serpentine and stepping onto the horse ride, John and Joe were a pleasing sight to any equestrian and as he lightly sprang into a trot, indeed even an extended trot life couldn't be better. There's something about an energetic and enthusiastic trot on a fresh day just out of the stable. The fresh air, the soft going, the rapidly approaching left hand bend, all seemed to be saying canter but Joe didn't seem to know canter. Throwing his head up and taking the bit between his teeth Joe hurtled into a flat out gallop heading West. The rapidly approaching left hand bend was a one hundred and eighty degree turn which would bring the rider round to an easterly facing direction running parallel to Kensington Gore.

It was at this point in the early morning haze John and Joe got their first sight of the crime scene some hundred yards ahead. It must have seemed a very odd sight to John as he rapidly approached the dark shapes of people apparently at prayer and fenced off by the soft blue and white marker tape of the

Metropolitan Police.

In no time at all both rider and horse were upon the hapless officers as they threw themselves to either side while Joe galloped through trailing 50 yards of tape across his breast and the loud booming public school accent exhorted them to "Get out of the way. I can't stop."

A somewhat bemused Detective Inspector in charge of the detail was later heard to wryly observe, 'I wouldn't have minded but half of the evidence had to be picked out of the horse's hooves half a mile down the ride by Hyde Park corner'.

Chapter Nineteen
Gift Horses And Casamayor

Over the years I have seen various Police authorities agree to finding the funds for setting up a Mounted Police unit within their respective force. Some would emerge as a small mounted unit only to be disbanded within a few years as Chief Constables couldn't find the funds to continue.

Horses cost a lot of money not just to purchase but also to maintain. Stables, forage, saddlery, veterinary care, training and regular monthly visits to the farriers all cost an amount which begs close scrutiny before embarking on such an expensive venture.

During the years I served it seemed that there was never any doubt that the Metropolitan Police Mounted Branch was regarded as a permanent requirement for policing London. The numbers had been set back in the 1920's as 201 horses working out of approximately twenty five stables. Some had an establishment of 20 horses while other stables only had three horses from as far afield as Chigwell in the North East to Epsom in the South, from Hammersmith and Richmond Park in the West to Bow and East Ham in the East.

The larger forces were similarly blessed with a mindset that a Mounted Branch was an essential part of policing their cities.

Manchester, Birmingham, Glasgow the City of London all had a heavy commitment to public order where police horses were an essential part of their law enforcement.

Nevertheless any opportunity to keep cost to a minimum was a constant requirement. On occasions we could be working a twelve, even a fifteen hour day but overtime payment was out of the question. Compensation would be given by 'Time in Lieu'. Even the stable manure was sold under contract. Slaughtered horses were sold for horse meat or processing for dog food. Old harness would be reprocessed and so on.

One great saving to be made was the acceptance of gift horses by the public. If a member of the public made an approach to the force offering a suitable mount we would be glad to accept and thereby make a considerable saving in purchase and training cost.

Such horses came from all walks of life from Racing Stables to privately owned mounts where the owner could no longer care for their horse either through cost or having to retire from riding.

Racing stables were a fairly frequent source of supply and during my time we accepted horses from famous trainers such as Jenny Pitman of Grand National and Gold Cup fame who would steer some owners into considering passing on suitable mounts to patrol London Streets.

I would receive a call from Jenny saying that a suitable mount was coming up for retirement and the owner would love to gift the horse to the police. On such occasions accompanied by experienced remount trainer 'Dicky Bird' we would travel down to assess the animal. Jenny was never wrong and several Mounts were gifted to the police.

Some owners would keep in contact and even come and visit their gift horses in their new environment. One such horse was an absolute godsend and the envy of any Mounted Officer lucky enough to be allocated such a mount.

'Casamayor', a finely bred twelve year old bay, imperious in demeanor, unruffled by any distraction either from crowd, missiles or traffic. A remarkable horse who had been trained by Peter Bailey. He had run in the Grand National in 1980 and 81. The form books show that he had the dubious distinction of falling twice in the 1980 National once without his rider. The facts are however that he successfully negotiated Beechers Brook twice before falling at the 29th Fence. He had been to America and won the 'Carolina Cup' in 1976 but the strangest thing was that when you schooled him he couldn't even trot over trotting poles or a cavalletti. He would bumble through it as though it wasn't there. Yet in a field of 30 or 40 horses thundering down toward a six foot high fence he could carry his rider safely over.

At the end of his racing career his owner recognized the wonderful qualities he had for crowd control and Police Duty and contacted us with his generous offer. He was easy to handle but somehow distant from all about him. He liked to be groomed but did not respond to a caress or word of comfort. He was on a different plane to the rest of us but a superb patrol horse and one that I envied for his reliability.

At the time I was serving as a Chief Inspector responsible for the stables and horses North of the Thames. My role often put me in charge of Mounted Police Units policing Wembley or public order (Disorder events) in Central London. To have a reliable horse was essential if one was required to lead into a violent or heavily congested crowd. Not a place for a nervous horse which might endanger the public and fail to lead a mounted contingent.

Casamayor had been allocated to Police Constable Nigel Harris at West Hampstead stables which came under my command. I had ridden him a couple of times at Wembley Stadium and was smitten by this lovely animal. Nigel, an accomplished horseman who knew he was onto a good thing was similarly impressed with him. I resorted to bribery to arrange a transfer by tempting him with a remount which he readily accepted. Hence the scene was set for me to have a most courageous, reliable and sensible mount for the coming disorders at the Wapping Printers' dispute.

Casamayor served me nobly for two years before gently collapsing and dying from a heart attack as he crossed Rotten Row on his return from the farriers in Knightsbridge Barracks. Police Constable Alvah Clarke a most competent and devoted Mounted

Picture by kind permission of Mike Pattison Photography, Hainault.

Police Horse Casamayor one time Grand National Runner.

Man of some 25 years experience explained to me the next day, 'He had just been re-shod and seemed perfectly normal as he stepped into the park. Walking calmly he just let out a sigh knelt down and gently rolled onto his side as I just stepped off him, no fuss and he was gone'.

Although still a reasonable age at 16 years it seemed as if the strain of all those years racing may have taken its toll. Either way he couldn't have chosen a more appropriate place to leave us.

Chapter Twenty

Southall Disorders, Blair Peach

If there was one demonstration that over the years I felt we were caught on the back foot, it was the events surrounding the proposed meeting of the National Front at Southall on the 23rd April 1979. The Anti Nazi League and other groups had clearly intimated their hostility to such a meeting and all the signs were one of confrontation.

During the days before, the Public Order Office had been working overtime in arranging sufficient police to maintain the peace. Mounted Branch were very much a part of these arrangements and ordered to assemble over 100 horses at a nearby disused Army Barracks for feeding and briefing. I was serving as Mounted Inspector at Hammersmith at the time and extremely fortunate in having a most experienced Sergeant, Sergeant Porter to assist me. We had travelled to the barracks by horse box and immediately fed our horses while taking our turn to be fed by the Police Catering department who always managed to produce a good meal in the most unlikely of situations.

The Superintendent was the Senior Mounted Officer in command of Mounted Branch and was a man not given to confiding with his Senior Officers until he delivered a full briefing to all the assembled officers in two separate batches. I could hear on the radio that things were rapidly deteriorating down in the Town Centre and suggested that we made moves to get into position and at least get our horses off the box.

The plan was that once the horses had been fed and we had

received our briefing we were to be transported by horse box over the short journey of about two miles to the Territorial Army Premises down by Hayes Bridge. For some reason the Superintendent didn't share my concern and calmly continued with the double briefing. We then climbed into our respective horse boxes before emerging on to the main roads to Southall where we spent the next hour in stationary traffic caused by the disorder down in the Town Centre.

We eventually arrived at the TA Barracks and were immediately instructed to 'Mount Up' before proceeding to the street at the back of Southall police station. The scene of devastation that greeted us as we crossed the junction with Lady Margaret Road was one of utter chaos. A burnt out double decker bus amazingly on its side and smashed shop windows were obvious. We saw Tariq Ali the main speaker for the Anti Nazi League on a flat roof top opposite the Town Hall where the National Front were meeting. The volume of the loud speakers was deafening as they sought to disrupt the meeting, yet amazingly the columns of Police horses calmly made their way under the cacophony of sound to their appointed positions.

We were divided into three or four separate sections of one Inspector one Sergeant and twenty Police Constables responding to instructions by personal radio. During the afternoon and evening we were moved from one location to another before eventually finding ourselves in a leafy back road where kindly residents brought out tea and biscuits.

Our final move was to the main Uxbridge Road on the west side of the Town Hall. Our role was to support a foot duty cordon in preventing further intrusion into the trouble spots caused by increasing numbers of Anti Nazi League supporters. After an initial push where some shop windows were broken the crowd started to disperse and our role was one of simply standing in line across the Uxbridge Road while things calmed down.

From my elevated position on horseback looking beyond the crowd and towards Uxbridge, maybe two hundred yards away, I could see what I could only describe as haphazardly abandoned

Special Patrol Group Carriers. They were empty, parked across the road while their respective crews were apparently engaged with demonstrators out of my sight down the side streets. I could hear on the radio that Mounted Branch were involved with crowd dispersal on the East side of the Town Hall but my serial were only involved by holding a line.

Eventually we were stood down in the back yard of Southall Police Station where after an hour or so we were dismissed. It was about one in the morning when we made our way back towards The TA Centre and I distinctly remember Sergeant Porter laughing as he looked behind us at a trail of over a hundred horses riding two abreast for what seemed like a world war one move up to the front.

It all seemed so surreal, even at that late hour there were many members of the public coming to their front gates and clapping as we passed. Some of our officers had been injured but my particular serial had seen no real violence, but one of the protestors, Blair Peach, had died in mysterious circumstance. We were all required to make statements of what action we had been involved in and what we had seen but we couldn't really help with any enquiry. The debate and speculation continue to this day.

Chapter Twenty One
Wembley Turf Used To Repair Scottish Lawns 1977

Nobody is more aware of the dangers created by uncontrolled crowd surges and crushes that can be caused by huge crowds in confined areas than those experienced by a mounted police officer.

Visual shots of overhead views from high vantage points or helicopters have no comparison when measured against the physical presence of being on horseback in a sea of humanity that occurs when hundreds if not thousands of people congregate in a confined area.

A mounted officer is often right in the thick of it but at the same time above it, whereas his foot duty colleagues while face to face with it will be unable to see the bigger picture or identify where the trouble might be caused.

Not only is the mounted officer well placed to see the trouble but has the means to direct the crowd away from the trouble spots and from his high vantage point able to move his horse within the crush and ease the pressure.

How many times over the years have we read of, or even been present at, situations where huge crowds have brought unbearable pressure upon a dividing wall or crowd barrier resulting in dreadful crush injuries or worse.

Not that a mounted police officer can't find themselves trapped in such a tight spot that they also cannot move. I have received reports at de-briefs following a busy game, where parents with children in arms were desperately beseeching mounted officers to 'Do something.'

The sorrow that we all feel when hearing of such disasters cannot compare with the trauma experienced by families of lost ones under such circumstances. The pain of the officers who have desperately tried to deal with an impossible situation and failed lives with them for a lifetime.

The best made plans and preparations can suddenly become inadequate as unexpected developments overtake the norm. Generally mounted officers would only deal with crowds outside the ground although on a rare occasion would be brought inside where trouble has surged onto the pitch. The mindless aggravation that can occur between opposing sides can create dangerous side effects not only to the mob but also to the innocent just looking for an enjoyable afternoon out with their family.

London has many major football stadiums capable of holding as many as eighty thousand spectators. In fact when I first joined the force in the late fifties it was not unusual to witness crowds in excess of a hundred thousand at the former Arsenal ground at Highbury. Of course most of the spectators were standing on the terraces where the placement of crush barriers prevented too much build up of weight and there was always the pitch itself which could serve as a safety valve as displayed by what became known as 'The White Horse Wembley' where Police Horse 'Billie' was to become so famous in the 1923 Cup Final.

It was the frequent pitch invasions that led to the introduction of secure fencing being erected at some of the major stadiums. This of course removed the safety measure created by being able to jump onto the pitch when the crush became unbearable as witnessed in the tragedy of Hillsborough where so many innocent lives were lost in 1989.

I can understand the pressure placed upon the Commander of any large event where immense crowd surges result in injury or worse. On one occasion I found myself trapped against one of the main entry points at Twickenham during the mid seventies. Normally Mounted Branch would only provide a small attendance at Twickenham, maybe just a Mounted Sergeant and three Constables. On this occasion of the Five Nations Rugby (as it was then) I was required to attend as the Mounted Inspector in charge of a mounted serial assisting with crowd control outside the ground.

The whistle had gone for kick off, when one of the main turnstiles adjacent to the coach and car park was suddenly besieged by coach loads of late comers. The crowds were desperate to get in rather than miss the match. They had travelled for hours to see this game but road congestion had delayed their arrival until after kick off. The gate staff were following instructions to check that each spectator had a ticket which led to a mindless push at the rear by the latecomers.

It was only by chance that I was at this particular point as most of the outside police presence had been stood down for refreshment. I could see this sudden late surge of arrivals was placing huge pressure not only on the gate staff but worse, the pressure on the poor souls at the front of the crowd. Children were being hoisted aloft as the pressure caused people to beg for relief. My horse and I were trapped against the exit gates as the position deteriorated. My shouts for reason and calm were ignored as the mindless crush from the back caused immense pressure against the doors and turnstile. Although I had called for assistance it seemed as though it would be too late to prevent serious injury to the people being crushed against the gate and walls.

From my viewpoint I could see over the eight foot high gate into the ground. The people inside were all seated unaware of the build up of spectators outside the ground. The spectators had taken their seats, all the gangways and entry point were clear and there was plenty of room to let the gates open. The ground inside and outside was level. To open the gates would allow the crowd through and relieve the unbearable pressure outside but there would be a surge. It was a decision I had to make quickly if on one hand we were to avoid crush injuries or worse, or allow a headlong uncontrolled surge on the other. On this occasion with the level ground and all seated we were able to open the gates safely and worked well thereby preventing crush injuries. Disaster could well have occurred had it been a situation where the ground was not level and gave way to crowded downhill terraces with standing spectators.

It was on the 4th June 1977 when the deciding match of the British Home Championship took place between England and Scotland at Wembley. For over a century this game regularly caused terrific emotions as the two sides met with 'The Auld Enemy' and the build up to the game had all the hall marks of a fiercely disputed game.

At the time I was serving as Mounted Inspector at West Hampstead, a posting which regularly required my attendance at major events at the old Wembley Stadium. As was normal in such cases a full briefing for the coming event was held under the auspices of Commander Don Sadler at Wembley Police Station during the week before. We received professional advice regarding intelligence received, various units were given their deployments for the day and as usual I submitted my suggested locations for the various postings of the Mounted Officers who were deployed outside the ground.

The Wembley turf was beautiful, with its immaculate lines of hallowed turf in bright contrast to the surrounding stands it was a groundsman's work of art. Definitely not a place for horses' hooves to carve out a divot and as such I had never known of police horses being on the pitch since the legendry match of what became known as 'The White Horse Wembley' of 1923.

There was enormous support from the Scottish Fans who had travelled down to Kings Cross in their thousands before taking the tube to Wembley Station. They were all in boisterous good humour and generally having a great time. Particularly so when they won the game two goals to one. Their ecstatic response led to them flooding onto the pitch in their thousands.

I was receiving reports from concerned fans leaving the ground regarding the absolute pandemonium that was taking place from within the ground when I received a direction from control to take all Mounted Officers and meet with Commander Sadler within the ground for further directions.

For the first time I entered the stadium through the main gates between the twin towers to be greeted by the deafening Wembley roar. The pitch was flooded with maybe twenty thousand fans who were rejoicing with raised Scottish scarves and flags. Some were balancing dangerously upon the crossbars of the goals while others were collecting handfuls of turf to take home as a memento. Mounted Police Sergeant Billy Waygood was already inside the ground with a small mounted force of about five officers and with the twenty or so that I had brought with me I met a concerned Commander Don Sadler who promptly asked what we could do to clear the pitch. A desperate plea from the groundsman to keep the horses off the pitch drew a smile as I surveyed the disappearing turf.

The sacred turf was no longer a concern and I hastily agreed with the Commander to form up in line at one end of the pitch together with foot duty officers to gradually sweep the fans towards the side track and stands.

In actual fact the foot duty were already doing a magnificent job with short lines of about ten officers with linked arms sweeping the mainly good natured fans ahead of them. As we moved down line abreast they joined us and to the cry of 'The pubs are open,' the fans made their way out of the arena complete with pieces of broken goal posts and pockets stuffed with Wembley turf.

Of course the press had a field day with dire reports of marauding hordes wantonly destroying the most prestigious of grounds and it was with considerable trepidation that I phoned the Commander's clerk the next day to arrange an interview.

I must confess that I felt somewhat inadequate in the measures we had taken to achieve the pitch clearance but with the benefit of hindsight we had played it just right. Together with the foot duty we had restored peace and sensible evacuation without any injuries or fatalities. The TV coverage showed us efficiently moving the crowd out of the ground and notwithstanding the desecration of the turf. All in all there was not anything more that we could have done.

Walking into Commander Sadler's office I could see the stress and concern that he had been going through. He was gracious in thanking the Mounted Branch in clearing the ground and congratulated us for the efficient evacuation. I in turn commended the foot duty for their good natured and efficient response and promised to pass on his comments to the mounted officers involved.

We both relaxed as we realized that despite the mindless hooliganism resulting in the pitch invasion the action taken by police was commendable.

As a humorous footnote I should mention that following the clearance of the pitch we returned to our various deployments around the stadium and whilst forming queues for the underground I observed two apparent workmen carrying a long set of double ladders down Olympic way towards the main road. They appeared cheerful and industrious as they went about their business under the curious eyes of thirty or so Mounted officers and probably over a hundred foot duty. It must have been some three or four minutes later that I heard over the radio a request from a crime conscious officer for a van to collect two prisoners with double ladders outside the underground station.

Chapter Twenty Two
Greenham Peace Camp And Cruise
Missiles.

London's Mounted Branch were rarely called upon to provide aid to other forces and even during the Miners' strike of 1984/85 we remained in London. While our provincial colleagues on horseback were being shipped around all the major coal mines assisting with disorders and picketing, our two hundred horses were kept in the Capital.

However there was one major change when we found ourselves being constantly ferried by horse box out to the Greenham Common American Air Force Base. For over a year during 1983 we constantly provided a mounted contingent of one Inspector, two Sergeants and twenty Constables as aid to an outside police force.

It was during the so called 'Cold War' with Russia when we were required to provide aid to the Thames Valley Police in their duties to prevent the base being invaded by the 'Peace Camp Ladies' who were protesting against the arrival and installation of cruise missiles containing nuclear warheads capable of reaching Russia. It was reported that each nuclear warhead was capable of delivering a destructive force of twenty times the strength of the Hiroshima and Nagasaki bombs.

The missile site itself covered 1000 acres of heath-land surrounded by twenty foot high wire mesh fencing topped with coils of razor wire. Within this area was an airfield with the longest concrete airstrip in Europe and many ghostly silos containing the dreaded nuclear missiles on transporters. Our role was to constantly patrol the perimeter fence during daylight hours to prevent the fences being breached by the protest women who were encamped all around the ground with many makeshift tent sites at each of the several gates.

Our horses were stabled at the nearby Newberry Race Course while we were accommodated at the Thames Valley Police Training School. Each contingent would perform a week's duty at a time before being relieved by the next consignment of Metropolitan Police Mounted Officers.

Our days were long and bitterly cold with twelve hour patrols. For the first time we were provided with exercise blankets to keep our horses warm. We could frequently dismount to ease our horse's backs but had to remain alert to respond to any threats to break into the Air Base.

It was amazing to see how these stout fences of wire mesh mounted on 'lamp post high' concrete stanchions could be breached by the determined rocking of 200 woman grasping the wire and rocking in unison before the post gave way.

Of course Military Personnel within the ground would soon arrive driving furiously up to the breach but by then the women would spread out within the ground to create mayhem.

The advantage of patrolling the fence on horseback was that we could get where no vehicles could. We were able to patrol through dense woodland along muddy trails impassable to vehicles.

We were in radio contact with a control point who could direct us to trouble spots or we could report a build up of pending trouble. It was misty and cold. Looking through the wire one could see the ominous presence of the gigantic silos that housed the missiles on their mobile carriers which added a sinister futuristic atmosphere to the scene.

But for the most part trouble would normally flare up outside the wire around the gates, where disruption would be caused when supply vehicles approached to provision the base.

The object of the Peace Camps was to demonstrate their objection and draw attention to the public of the dangers of nuclear war and the existence of the base. For the most part we had a good natured relationship with these tough ladies who came from all walks of life. Their ages ranged from children in pushchairs right the way through to Senior Citizens. TV crews and press photographers were everywhere as they arranged their protest.

At times their numbers exceeded thirty thousand as they encircled the miles of wire holding hands and singing protest songs. The makeshift tents appeared in their hundreds. Initially there were no toilet facilities and on occasion bailiffs were breaking up their camps and removing their sleeping bags and cooking facilities. Field kitchens appeared and well wishers were constantly dropping off supplies as they showed their support for this stalwart group of protesters.

Along with many other officers I found an empathy with their mindset and quite often found the discussion and exchanges helped to pass the time as they made a fuss of our horses. For over a year we provided aid to Thames Valley Police. Our constant heath-land patrols and ability to react and get to difficult terrain was a welcome break from performing crowd control duties at Tottenham and Arsenal, in truth, I think some officers were sorry when our assistance was no longer required.

Chapter Twenty Three
Dreadful Carnage In The Park

No matter whatever the weather you could always rely on the park to lift your spirits once you got out into the fresh air. I was in a most privileged position in being able to select my own route for a three hour patrol and on one occasion, 20th July 1982. I decided to head off for the North ride and Bayswater Road with a view to emerging at Marble Arch and then on into Oxford Street.

As I stepped out of the park I heard the most unmistakable sound of a bomb detonating. From my angle it seemed to come from the direction of the Palace and looking southwards I could see a pall of brown smoke rising from a point around Hyde Park Corner. It was at a time when the media were making much fuss about some revelation regarding alleged recordings of private telephone conversations of members of the Royal Family and for a few seconds my thoughts bizarrely were 'What now' when over the radio came the shocking news that The Queen's Life Guard had been attacked by a car bomb.

Quickly returning to the stable and changing to my car I drove the short distance to Serpentine Road from where I ran the last hundred yards over the Dell Bridge into South Carriage Drive where the horrific aftermath of the bomb was revealed.

As I write these notes some 30 odd years later some details are confused with the passing of time. But the awful images of that day will stay with me forever. The fallen horses, the injured and lifeless bodies of both horses and men, the ambulances, the horses that could walk being led back towards the barracks all made for a devastating scene that hadn't been seen since the first world war.

My first concern was for the two mounted police officers who were escorting the Queen's Life Guard. Traditionally the Household Cavalry were always escorted by two mounted officers who would facilitate their progress through traffic along the South Carriage Road and Hyde Park Corner on their route to Horse Guards Parade. Normally these officers would have come from the stables in Hyde Park but whenever they were short of staff the horses and riders were supplied from the police stables at Hammersmith. Such was the case on this fateful day. Police Constables Paul Ryan and John Davies supplied the escort riding police horses 'Yeti' and 'Echo' and found themselves in a nightmare of devastation and carnage.

Amazingly Paul Ryan who had been leading the escort was able to ride over to where I stood and calmly report that John Davies had been injured by shrapnel and taken to hospital while his horse Echo had been taken to the stables in Hyde Park Barracks.

I cannot express enough my admiration for this young constable who had experienced a most horrific event. The shock of the explosion of the car bomb just seconds after he had ridden past it, the sight he had immediately witnessed once he had calmed his horse must have all added to a desperate feeling of wanting to help. Yet here he was, still able to assess the situation and report on the whereabouts of his colleague and horse. Paul and Yeti had not been struck by any debris and were physically unharmed though what turmoil was going through his mind could only be guessed at. I was concerned for his welfare but with commendable courage he was able to return to the nearby stables.

In the meantime making my way over the short distance to the barracks found 'Echo'. In the lower stable area where many soldiers were holding bloodied swabs to various wounds on several horses, who, in spite of all the turmoil, were happily munching on haynets.

I found a young trooper holding Echo on a stable head collar. He was able to point out many shrapnel wounds. Although showing no sign of pain Echo obviously needed early assessment and veterinary attention. Looking round I found many other horses also needing attention and went to seek out the veterinary officer.

I didn't have to look far when I found Major Noel Carding miraculously saving the life of one of his charges by stitching up the windpipe of cavalry horse 'Sefton'. I could see that he would be some time in spite of his assurances that he would be able to deal with all the injured horses in time. I volunteered to call up more vets and went in search of the Adjutant to gain permission to draft in more help. Understandably the Adjutant was out but I was ushered into the Commanding Officer's office by a most helpful clerk where Colonel Andrew Parker Bowles readily agreed to my suggestion of calling in more vets.

As I passed through the Colonel's outer office I was greatly saddened by the site of the ladies gathered there waiting for news of their soldier husband's fate. A most grievous moment as I realized the anguish they must be going through.

I was grateful to be able to do something useful and quickly arranged for the urgent attendance of our own vet and The King's Troop Veterinary Officer from the nearby Royal Tournament at Earls Court. The rest of my day was taken up with reports from the Mounted Branch perspective. (All injuries sustained by Police Horses and veterinary treatment had to be submitted through the Chief Superintendent's office) and visiting a cheerful John Davies in hospital.

John was sitting up in bed with his arm in a sling. Attended by his lovely wife Karen, John could only explain that one moment he was riding at the tail end of the escort and then found himself sitting on the grass. He was unaware that the flying shrapnel had passed through his left arm bicep and it was miraculous that he and Echo hadn't been killed. Examination of his horse and the wrecked saddle wallets was evidence that he had literally lived through a hail of lethal flying debris.

That day four soldiers and seven horses of the Blues and Royals had been murdered by the IRA many more had been badly injured, a further seven soldiers of the band of the Royal Green Jackets had also lost their lives in an explosion under the bandstand in Regents Park. Miraculously both John Davies and Paul Ryan had survived the most horrendous event to occur in the country since the blitz.

Chapter Twenty Four

'They Shoot Horses Don't They?'

During the week following the Hyde Park and Regents Park atrocities much press coverage was quite rightly given to the miraculous courage and recovery of 'Sefton' the trooper's horse who had been so magnificently saved by the prompt action of the veterinary officer Major Noel Carding. In the meantime police horse Echo was receiving daily attention to his wounds from the soldiers of the Household Cavalry in his unaccustomed accommodation in Knightsbridge Barracks.

It was during this period that in my capacity as Chief Inspector I was required to accommodate a press launch for the charity RADAR. 'The Royal Association for Disability Rehabilitation.'

On the same day that the much recovered police horse Echo was led from Knightsbridge Barracks across to the police stables in Hyde Park, a press and publicity launch was to take place in the police station yard. The press and photographers were on scene while a pretty young disabled rider was mounted on a police horse accompanied by a mounted gunner from the 'King's Troop Royal Horse Artillery' in full ceremonial dress. This little pageant was accompanied by 'The voice of TV show jumping' Dorian Williams and film star Anthony Andrews.

Police Sergeant Wally Davies and myself stood by while the people involved arranged the scene for the photographers. Rosettes were presented, and posters revealed while the cameras clicked away when the event organisers inquired if 'Echo' could be involved in the photo shoot. Battle scarred Echo was duly brought out and played his part in promoting this wonderful charity when one of the Press asked if we could arrange for Echo's rider to be present.

The police press bureau had no objection to this and I felt that if it could add to the charity's appeal then so much the better. While we were waiting for John Davies to arrive the press got wind of a good story and picture opportunity. The yard was rapidly filling up with reporters and photographers when the young, blond headed constable John Davies arrived with his arm in a sling following his bomb injury. John and Echo were reunited for the first time since the blast and the picture of John blowing on Echo's wrinkled muzzle made all the national front pages the next day.

Picture, Copyright Metropolitan Police Intellectual Property.

Mounted Police Constable John Davies
reunited with Police Horse Echo
one week after the Hyde Park Bombing.
Note the shrapnel wounds in Echo's neck and underbelly.

It was wonderful publicity for the Mounted Police and I thought the picture would add to the publicity for the charity. The PR people from RADAR were more doubtful and worried that their charity might take second place to the appeal of the wounded horse and rider. As it turned out the launch was a great success although it was to lead to events which I never expected.

Within two days of making the front pages of the national press my office became inundated with sackfuls of fan mail for Echo. Beautiful cards had painstakingly been produced by children of all ages accompanied by packets of mints and cube sugar. Bags of apples and carrots appeared at the stable door from well wishers. Visitors and well wishers were turning up at the stable door for a sight of the hero horse. Cheques, cash and even Postal Orders were arriving daily and as it was police policy to acknowledge every letter from the public it soon became apparent that a dedicated team would have to take over the mail for a few days.

It was during this time of euphoric support for 'Echo' that I received a call from the front office informing me that a reporter from the press was asking for me. Making my way to the front desk I was met by a rather cold looking individual who having produced his I/D and reluctantly shaking hands started to ask questions regarding 'Echo's' welfare. He declined my invitation to come to my office claiming that he just wanted to know what would happen to 'Echo'.

I explained that we had no reason to doubt that the horse would make a complete recovery and that once all his wounds were healed Echo would gradually be brought back into work. 'And then?' He asked somewhat belligerently. I remained helpful but picked up the vibes that this individual was not good news. 'What happens then after a lifetime of loyal service? He asked. There was no getting away from it other than to suggest a formerly arranged interview at a later date which would only be seen as a prevarication. 'Well, you obviously know our policy of retiring our horses once they become incurably lame or diseased to such an extent that it becomes cruel to keep them alive; they are humanely destroyed.'

I then spent the next ten uncomfortable minutes explaining how, in common with the rest of the equine world in the country, the Metropolitan Police resorted to use of the humane killer to dispatch incurably sick and injured horses in cases where it would be cruel to keep them alive.

I was merely stating the facts and somewhat uncomfortably stating the Metropolitan Police's policy at the time. My mind drifted off to times when during serving in the army and later in the police where horses had to be put down. Times where I had witnessed the destruction of these lovely horses, beautifully groomed and in good condition in all respects other than to be suffering from the hideous effects of laminitis, emphysema or other incurable condition.

It was a sound policy and for a country which had heavily relied upon horse transport and the use of horses both in every day life and on the battle fields of Europe for centuries, not an unacceptable one to the public at large. Had they been asked what should be done with crippled and mutilated horses in permanent pain, most would agree that humane euthanasia was the right thing to do. Of course it didn't help our case and seemed uncaring that the payment we received for the animal's carcass by the horse slaughter would be recycled into the horse purchase budget.

Indeed one of the forms to be carried by every constable on the beat was form 29 specifically designed to get a vet's signed agreement that it would be inhumane to keep the horse alive for a moment longer than necessary before they were destroyed.

But in 1982 times were changing. The public no longer saw horses on a daily basis and the majority had never had any dealings with horses at all. Consequently following my uncomfortable interview with the unfriendly reporter at the front office desk, I wasn't surprised to see the headline the next day in large print the accusation 'They shoot horses, don't they?' which also happened to be the title of a current film.

The Mounted Branch found themselves fending off allegations of callous indifference to our equine servants. Nothing could be further from the truth but unsurprisingly the sacks of fan mail arriving in my office were considerably tempered by letters alleging heartless cruelty. I answered all these letters myself and hopefully allayed the public's concern.

But there was a happy conclusion to the foregoing events and I must agree that the tricky reporter at the front desk actually did us a power of good. Following a week of responding to the public's concern both by local radio and letters regarding our procedure for disposal of our retired horses, we changed our policy completely.

Many offers of public support came in offering homes for our ageing and infirm horses where the public guaranteed that they would provide constant care, including medicines, exercise and green fields. Such offers were closely vetted to ensure that no abuse of our horses was likely. If their offer was accepted, it was to be on the understanding that they took full responsibility for the rest of the animal's life. Ironically in such cases the final demise resulted in the animal being put down in the same manner as they would have been in the police, but at   least they could enjoy a period of rest and green fields before the inevitable.

In Sefton and Echo's cases, both were retired to the home of Rest provided by the horse sanctuary at Speen Farm. A wonderful facility in Buckinghamshire funded by voluntary donation, this peaceful location set in the rolling hills of the Chilterns provided a beautiful home during the final years of our faithful servants.

Both Echo and Sefton received much adulation from visitors to Speen Farm before finally passing away in their 30's.

A happy conclusion to a most outrageous attack.

Chapter Twenty Five

The Mets War Horses

Of The 70's and 80's

As I write these memoirs some twenty years after I retired in 1994, I think back to those moments when death and injury occurred on the streets of London.

The loss of life and particularly the loss of horses remind me of the terrible suffering that Soldiers and their horses suffered during the First World War and realise how fortunate our generation has been in not suffering the trials of warfare.

More recently we have been reminded of those dreadful times by the medium of film and stage in the production of 'Warhorse', a haunting account portraying trench warfare, barbed wire and devastation. The foregoing two chapters refer to our own experiences in terrorist situations in which our horses suffered bomb blasts and the resulting chaos in London.

But there were other bomb incidents involving Police Horses, mainly unknown to the public. I recorded the following article for the Mounted Branch in house magazine 'One One Ten' in 2014. Edited and produced by retired Sergeant and one time Mounted Branch Museum Curator Chris Forester it catches the desperate mood of the times and reveals how our horses were also caught up in such events.

The Met's War Horses of the 70's and 80's

During the IRA Bombings of London in the 1970's and 80's it wasn't unusual to hear an explosion while on Mounted Patrol. None more so than when John Davis and Paul Ryan were escorting the Household Cavalry along the South Carriage Road in Knightsbridge where the IRA detonated a car bomb. The courage and fortitude of those two officers and their horses during and following that horrific event will stay with me forever.

It seemed that Mounted Branch Officers were often involved in such events. Something that John Smith and I were discussing at last year's reunion. Without doubt the Hyde Park Bombings were the most traumatic and hit our horses hardest while on mounted duties but the other incident that we remembered was the bombing of Great Scotland Yard in 1973.

It was the day of the Mounted Branch dinner and dance, a grand affair to be held at the Hyde Park Hotel. I was stationed at Kings Cross, posted 9am to 5pm and on my way in from patrol and just crossing Penton Rise when I heard a distant explosion. As I made my way into the station yard I heard another almighty explosion from about a mile away. Immediately control came over the radio that Commander instructs every available man to make their way down to the Old Bailey. You've never seen a horse turned in so quickly as I grabbed the stable first aid kit and jumped in a car just leaving the yard. The scene at the Old Bailey was devastating with shards of glass from the high rise buildings stacked up to three or four feet high. But down at Great Scotland Yard there was another drama unfolding.

I was unaware but the first explosion I had heard was from a car bomb left outside the stables in Great Scotland Yard. John King had been senior officer on duty at GY that day and PS John Smith was his Sergeant. There had been an authenticated message from Cannon Row that a bomb was about to be detonated right outside the stables and John King surely had a tale to tell about the incident and its aftermath.

It doesn't seem possible that it was over 40 years ago but surely something that would be of interest to our new readers. John Smith suggested we should get together so, 2 Months later, together with Mike Walker we all met at the King's house in Twickenham.

We were warmly welcomed by John's wife Joyce and were soon enjoying coffee and biscuits while the Two Johns talked us through those moments of terror and subsequent recovery which was like something out of the wartime Blitz.

JK now in his 80's but well recovered from his virus took up the story by explaining that JS had just gone off early turn duty. JK was in the front office at Great Scotland Yard when he received a call from Cannon Row police station to say that they had just received a coded message believed to be from the IRA that a car bomb parked outside the building was due to explode at 3pm.

It was too late to evacuate the building and gave John just 25 minutes to move all personnel to the basement and transfer the horses from the front stable to the rear. John explained that the Mounted Branch Admin Staff (PS Ron Gower and PC), The Diplomatic Protection Squad, Three Canteen staff and Two Traffic Wardens were all taking cover in the basement boiler room below stairs while John, Norman Hart and Bob Puffett moved all the horses from the front stable to the rear stable where they crowded into the aisle behind the tethered horses. There wasn't enough room for all the horses so Norman held one horse on the coconut matting on the ramp but immediately under the large glass roof that served for inner light inside the building. Sergeant Smith's horse Peggy was renowned for her kicking and couldn't stand near other horses so she had to take her chances in the front stable with her back to the street windows.

And then they waited...... and waited..., with the clock ticking. With ten minutes to go John had a quick look outside the yard door and saw an army vehicle come to an abrupt halt by a vehicle not 30 yards from the front door. An Army Major and Sergeant jumped from the vehicle and after a quick inspection ran back to the car and made off at high speed.

By now all of Whitehall, Great Scotland Yard and Horse Guards were all in lock down with roads cordoned off and traffic stilled. The atmosphere was electric with terrified staff in the basement, Norman and Bob standing to their horse's heads and John in the front office under the table making frantic calls to nearby stables to arrange support in anticipation of the forthcoming explosion.

JK. 'There was a flash of light closely followed by a crumph and then a cascading sound of the glass roof and framework crashing to the floor some three floors below where part of the car engine had fallen through the roof. The personnel sheltering in the basement must have been terrified as they waited for the glass to stop falling. I was safe under the table but all the plaster ceiling and neon lights had fallen around me. Norman and Bob had managed to hang on to their horses but Peggy had received shards of glass in her haunches from the in-blown stable windows.'

'Outside was the Blitz all over again with fallen glass burning cars and wrecked buildings. The roads were full of debris and our own inner yard smothered in fallen glass tangled iron struts and bits of car.'

John Smith then took up the story. 'I'd had the most dreadful day imaginable, there was a tube strike on and free parking was available in London so I had taken my car which promptly broke down after half a mile. I then had to walk eight miles from Richmond to GY to be bollocked for being late. It's funny but as I approached GY that day I just felt that there was a bomb there, was it sixth sense, had I subconsciously picked up on the news that a car bomb had been defused outside New Scotland Yard? I don't know, but the fact is during that morning I had ridden Peggy right by that car full of explosives as we all did. Apparently the IRA had meant to leave it outside the recruiting depot but found the granting of free parking during the tube strike meant early commuters had already taken their preferred space.'

'When my shift was finished and with no means of transport Pete Saunders came over from Hyde Park and got me home by 3pm. No sooner was I indoors when the phone rang. It was Norman

Hart saying 'You'd better get back Sarge, Mr King could do with some help.'

'With no transport running and my car broken down I grabbed my wife's bike and pedalled my way back along the 10 miles to GY before collecting a puncture outside the Albert Hall where once again I found myself walking to GY for the second time that day.'

While John Smith was cycling and walking back to GY John King realised that the stables were no longer habitable. JK then received another call from Cannon Row to say that her Majesty the Queen had sent message to say that the Royal Mews was available for any horses that needed accommodation. The street outside was a nightmare with fallen glass, masonry and wrecked cars. However the council were very quickly upon the scene and rapidly clearing the streets. Inside GY the glass on the ramp and leading to the entrance had to be cleared to enable the horses to be led out. By now aid had arrived from other stables and working parties were clearing debris from the ramp and floor to provide an exit. (Note, Health and Safety.... further falls of Debris? Not on this occasion, just get on with it.)

JK continued, 'At about 4pm Chief Superintendent Albert (Badgy) Pilcher arrived and instructed that horses should move to the Royal Mews immediately. We discussed waiting while things settled down but Badgy felt we should move immediately. Officers were doing the best they could in a wrecked tack room trying to identify the right tack to different horses.'

JS. 'Having got everyone mounted I led out of GY on foot and in plain clothes to The Royal Mews via Cannon Row, and Rochester Row. No sooner had we got out into Great Scotland Yard when I heard a kerfuffle behind. Looking back I can remember poor PC Murphy whose horse had fallen resulting in him sustaining a fractured pelvis and needing an ambulance. Eventually we got going again and I led the way to Rochester Row where we dropped off some horses, then on to The Royal Mews and Finally Hyde Park Stables to complete my walk of some 25 miles that day.'

JK. 'At last everything had been sorted, stable and offices evacuated, the building closed down. It was supposed to be the day of the Mounted Branch Dinner and Dance at the Hyde Park Hotel but there was no way I could get there in time for 7.30pm. Then Assistant Commissioner John Gerrard arrived to inspect the damage, he was adamant that I would go to the ball and promptly dispatched his chauffeured car to collect my wife from home and convey her to the Dinner and instructed me to attend in my hacking jacket.'

Aftermath.

The stables at Great Scotland Yard were completely rebuilt with a far better glass and laminated wood canopy.

The GY stores and medicine cupboard received a vastly improved stock following John King's creative writing and assessment of the losses.

Sadly PC Murphy injuries were so serious that he could not return to Mounted Duties.

The glass splinters in police horse Peggy's haunches had to stay there until they worked their own way out because nobody could get near her.

Ten terrorist of the IRA were arrested at Heathrow trying to board planes for Dublin that same day.

John King was commended for his prompt action and did get to the ball in his hacking jacket which was a black tie job.

John Smith arrived for early turn on time the next morning.

Article presented by Andy Petter Mounted Branch 1962 to 1994

Chapter Twenty Six
Wapping, Crowd Dispersal And Its
Aftermath

The actual dispersal of the mob at Wapping on the 24th January 1987 couldn't have been more straightforward and in accordance with the guidelines as laid down by the Home Office for such a dispersal.

Police lines had been formed and were clearly apparent. Business premises were being protected from law breakers intent on preventing law abiding citizens getting to their place of work.

Numerous injuries were being sustained by officers and civilians alike as the mob element within the crowd indiscriminately bombarded them with a non-stop hail of missiles. Attempts to overturn vehicles and set them alight all contributed to a realisation that the Police were losing control of a situation which had been deteriorating over a period of two hours.

Snatch squads had attempted to remove the ringleaders, Officers with long shields had been replaced with a line of normally dressed beat bobbies with short shields in an attempt to defuse the situation (Quickly replaced with the more protective long shields as many injuries were taking the officers out of the line).

The whole scene was descending into chaos when the decision to use Mounted Branch to push back the rioters was taken. Several announcements were made to warn the crowd of our intent and 'please leave the scene.' These instructions were completely ignored and probably not even heard as the mob sensed victory.

The Ground Commander had warned me some twenty minutes before we were deployed that we were to relieve the shield serials but this order had been put on hold pending the arrival of the Deputy Assistant Commissioner who wanted to see the situation for himself. Once he arrived we got the nod and myself and the shield serial Chief Inspector took over.

All our years of training and experience kicked in as our wonderful horses moved through the police line and pushed the mob back. The well rehearsed movement of foot duty officers separating and leaving the path clear to approach the closely packed rioters at a strong trot caused them to fall back as they fled.

I caught the eye of the shield serial Chief Inspector, I looked either side to my Mounted Serial. They had removed their high visibility jackets leaving me as the only bright centre point on which to control the advance. The mounted officers were well briefed and my immediate objective was to clear the ground of hooligans in the Highway. A signal from me and the foot duty shield serial parted to right and left. Over twenty horses, line abreast, surged into the Highway and across into Wellclose Street.

The mob were well prepared, the hail of debris was astonishing and non-stop as the bricks first hit Casamayor's protective visor and then my visor and body armour. It has to be said that this sort of action, although part of our training and something that had been rehearsed during our regular shield training exercises at Hounslow, was completely unusual in its intensity.

Ninety nine per cent of our duties resolved around day to day patrols, meeting and communicating with the public, visits to schools and putting on displays at fetes and gymkhanas. Any violence we experienced on a regular basis was to be found in keeping warring opponents apart at local football derbies such as Tottenham versus Milwall or Chelsea versus West Ham.

On this occasion there was to be no gentle clearance of mass crowds by use of gentle half passes as our horses moved quietly into a peaceful crowd, this was a case of a well rehearsed tactic using well trained officers and horses who had been ordered, and then led, into a trouble seeking mob of reckless law breaking

132

hooligans enjoying an opportunity to break down law and order and prevent law abiding citizens getting to their place of work.

Crossing the highway at a strong trot the waves of hooligans fell back and fled as we moved into Wellclose Street. Virtually all the Mounted Officers knew the ground well. Both myself and my Inspector had walked the streets prior to the event to familiarize ourselves with the lay out.

We knew the room for clearance was limited and I knew we couldn't enter Wellclose Street very far before I would call a halt to prevent crushing. Raising my right hand and coming to a halt line abreast we became a static target for the mob on the green to our right and left. By raising my arm I had exposed the unprotected underarm of my body and suffered broken ribs from a house brick and damaged left hand from a piece of iron railing. However we had achieved our objective and relieved the attacks on the shield serials and so were able to withdraw.

Wellclose Street was quite a steep rising ground and from my position I could clearly see down into the highway where I witnessed the alarming sight of one Police Constable virtually unconscious as his horse carried him back to our starting point in Virginia Street at the canter.

On the face of it our objective had been achieved. The movement from start to finish had taken less than a minute, there was minimum damage to the public and the road was clear of rioters. As we made a controlled retreat I could see a broad grin on the face of the Shield Serial Chief Inspector as he approached me lifting his visor. For more than two hours his officers had suffered numerous injuries. They had switched from peaceful mode to defence and finally deployed for crowd dispersal. From a seemingly frightening and helpless position they had witnessed the Mounted Branch taking control of the street and enabled them to regain the initiative.

There was still some disorder but a second approach at the walk we made calm progress as the crowd dispersed and I found myself at the top of the hill close to the Union bus that served as a control and meeting point for the union officials. We were still inviting targets for the mob who mindlessly hurled any item they could find at us. Rocks and bricks were mainly missing their targets and the bus itself was taking many hits.

The remainder of that evening was spent in moving the remaining demonstrators along the highway and away from the bedlam. Injury reports both to men and horses were completed. Wounds were dressed or in a few cases officers were taken to hospital but nobody, police or public were seriously hurt. It was a most successful example of restoring order from a rapidly descending situation and returning to a peaceful mode.

Not that you would have thought it from the subsequent press reports and formal inquiry that followed for weeks and months after the event. For the truth was that the police had been caught up within a dispute between the Print unions and Rupert Murdoch's answer to the Spanish practices experienced in Fleet Street, which was simply to move the whole works to Wapping and start again.

Police officers were not political animals and if they did hold any personal views they did not impinge upon their duty. For more than a year they had regularly turned out at the dead of night to keep the approaches to Wapping open for normal access by the workforce. The 24th January 1987 had become a focal point for Union action. It was supposed to be a peaceful demonstration but had descended into a riot.

The criticism leveled against police particularly in the article from The Haldane Society entitled 'A case to Answer' showed a naivety which failed to take into account the dangers that would follow if the police had lost control of the situation. Fortress Wapping as it was known could not have withstood the onslaught that would have followed in the event of Police losing control of the streets. Some estimates of that night put the crowd as being in excess of twenty thousand most of whom were exercising their right to demonstrate and unaware of the violence in The Highway.

On a personal note I was immensely proud of the mounted officers and their horses. No long mounted issue truncheons had been used and once the mob were broken up the crowds were persuaded to leave the scene as one would have done at a football match. Their resolute and calm behaviour demonstrated great professionalism under extreme provocation but due to the politics involved never received the recognition they deserved.

In the following months Mounted Officers continued with their duties in a cheerful manner and to my knowledge showed no concern regarding the outcome of the Northamptonshire police inquiry into our conduct. The legal advice given to all officers was to make no statement unless a case was made against them although as officer in charge I made a full and detailed statement to the enquiry team which apparently was very helpful and prevented the Press saying we were being evasive. I was glad to do so, as were a couple of others, we had nothing to hide and were content in the knowledge that we had performed our duty professionally and ensured the rights of law abiding citizens to attend their place of work. My sister Margaret was at last able to sleep at night and stop worrying about her brother.

The final report in the article headed 'Wapping Violence' which appeared in the Times on the 16th February 1990 refers to the rejection by Scotland Yard to the criticisms by the report and that, from The Mounted Branch perspective, was the end of the matter.

Chapter Twenty Seven
Dog Section, Retirement And The Future

I eventually went on to become Superintendent responsible for not only London's Mounted Branch but also London's Dog Section for my final year before retirement in 1994. I had always admired the Dog Section tremendously; indeed, had I not been accepted for Mounted Branch, the Dog Section was my next choice. It was a privilege to see the training and professionalism under the guidance of Chief Inspector Alan Clarke that went into producing an obedient but responsive, mainly Alsatian, force of dogs and dog handlers for London's streets.

The specialist dog unit based at Nine Elms and directed by Chief Inspector Ian Hunt was constantly in demand for drug and explosive substance searches. They provided great security for state occasions and VIP meetings. I was privileged to see spaniels trained to detect explosive substances performing a roadside test actually point to Semtex that had been buried in the road or hidden on aircraft.

The Dog Section was, and still is, a great crime fighting force. Their ability to track scents from a scene of crime and follow the culprit's trail is a great asset to law enforcement. The Metropolitan Police had over 300 dog handlers working across London.

As a police cadet in 1956 I served for a six month period at Traffic Division at Bow in the East End. I would often go out on patrol with the cars and on one occasion found that we had a dog handler on board complete with Alsatian. As a young lad up from the country I had a good rapport with all animals and happily agreed to take part in a training exercise where I would pretend to be a fleeing criminal. It seemed that as a nimble seventeen year old I was ideal for such an exercise and the Alsatian in question was wagging its tail furiously as I put a protective sleeve around my arm. I was given a fifty yard start and would run flat out until brought down by my over enthusiastic new found friend.

This all came back to me some thirty or so years later when, upon returning to the stables at Hyde Park having accompanied the Duke of Kent on a practice ride for the Trooping the Colour Ceremony, we encountered a smart dog handler with his Alsatian carrying a protective training sleeve. We both laughed at the dog's enthusiasm whereupon his handler said 'Fancy running for my dog Gov?' Memories of a happy youth came back as I surprised him by saying I would.

I should have guessed, the word quickly got round the station that there was an idiot Mounted Branch Chief Inspector taking off his spurs and donning a protective sleeve while preparing to run for the dog section. The handler became impressively serious as he briefed me for the forthcoming chase and instructed me to stop the second the dog grabbed my arm but to remain standing while he would try and get the dog to let go. 'Try and get him to let go, he won't bite my arse, will he?' This didn't seem to be going the same way as my earlier experience in the East End but the dog was still tail wagging and I could see a small group gathering including the Duke by the yard entrance. I had to go through with it or lose face. 'Don't look back, hold your arm out and run like stink,' was my final instruction as I raced down the slope away from the station. 'Stop or I will release the dog.' came the clear voice of the chasing instructor. This sequence of events and warning was clearly a Dog Section trick as I immediately heard the snarling growl of my attacker as he grabbed my arm and hung on. But I was impressed with the rapid response to the handlers command 'Leave' when the dog let go and continued to wag his tail. We shook hands and received a round of applause for this cameo performance as we returned to the stables. It was one of those magic moments which crop up impromptu in life and provides an enrichment which cannot be planned but is long remembered after the event.

To locate, purchase and allocate puppies was a constant requirement for maintaining an ongoing dog unit. Training courses were producing classes virtually on a monthly basis. In addition to purchases from the public, the Met had their own dog breeding program to ensure we produced enough dogs to sustain a regular force.

Metropolitan Police Dog Section.
Winners of the 1993 National Police Dog Trials.
Pictured with Police Commissioner Sir Peter Imbert and
Superintendent Andy Petter

I was extremely fortunate in serving at a time when we hosted the 34th National Police Dog Trials during April 1993 and for the Metropolitan Police Dog Section to win the Championship was the icing on the cake.

But the times were changing. Various departments were undergoing severe scrutiny in the 'Nothing Sacred Review' crime units were being reduced or closed completely as the scrutiny identified more streamlined and economical measures to operate.

Both Dog Sections and then Mounted Branch came under the searching studies of the Scrutineers as they made recommendations for cut backs and civilianization. In 1994 the Mounted Branch still had its original establishment of 201 horses and 210 officers which was the same strength that had been decided back in the 1920's. There were 20 stables attached to stations throughout London. Some stables only had room for four horses while the larger stables at Bow, Hammersmith, Wandsworth, Rochester Row and Great Scotland Yard had space for eighteen or more.

Inevitably the scrutinizers recommended stable closures and reductions by more than thirty per cent with great emphasis on introducing civilian grooms in the mistaken belief that such measures would enable officers to patrol for longer periods in the belief that the civilians could groom and care for the stables and horses.

This of course was a nonsense and I responded to their recommendations pointing out that it wasn't unusual to turn out over 120 horses on public order events on weekends and that although horses could and did patrol for long periods on special events, to do so on a daily basis would soon see an increase in lameness, officers would have no horses to ride while they watched their newly placed civilian grooms looking after sick horses. I was glad to see the Branch retained its establishment at 201 horses up to the time I retired in 1994.

Nevertheless, since I retired the branch has been reduced to 120 horses working from eight stables. The Annual two day Metropolitan Police Horse Show has been abandoned in the interest of economy, though the highly regarded Activity Ride still performs at 'Olympia' and similar events. Civilianization has come and gone as further economies were made and surprise, surprise, officers have gone back to caring for their own horses and stables.

There's no doubt that the Police Service has undergone revision and severe cutbacks which includes Mounted Branch and Dog Sections particularly in London. Nevertheless, regardless of the reduced numbers, the advantage of a high profile police officer patrolling on horseback at a pace where easy communication with the public is possible will always be of enormous benefit to policing.

The main purpose of a police service will always be the maintenance of law and order and the preservation of peace. There's no doubt that the political scene has changed in relation to public disorder to a point where other methods of crowd dispersal will be favoured in place of using horses. But the role of using Mounted Branch for policing large crowds and general patrol will remain a constant policing tool.

Over the years Mounted Officers struck up a wonderful rapport with their mounts and such was their affection that some officers even delayed their retirement until their allocated horse came up for retirement as well, leaving them to ride off into the sunset together.

As I look back over a lifetime of working with horses for Military and Police work, I realize I have been witness to a wonderful organization which leaves me with many fond memories. I can only be grateful for the comradeship and wonder at the good service horses and dogs provide with their courage even their vices, and the privilege it was to serve in the Metropolitan Police Service.

End